Penguin Specials fill a gap. Written by some of today's most exciting and insightful writers, they are short enough to be read in a single sitting – when you're stuck on a train; in your lunch hour; between dinner and bedtime. Specials can provide a thought-provoking opinion, a primer to bring you up to date, or a striking piece of fiction. They are concise, original and affordable.

To browse digital and print Penguin Specials titles, please refer to **penguin.com.au/penguinspecials**

LOWY INSTITUTE

The Lowy Institute is an independent, nonpartisan international policy think tank. The Institute provides high-quality research and distinctive perspectives on the issues and trends shaping Australia's role in the world. The Lowy Institute Papers are peer-reviewed essays and research papers on key international issues affecting Australia and the world.

For a discussion on *India in a World Adrift*, visit the Lowy Institute's daily commentary and analysis site, *The Interpreter*: **www.lowyinstitute.org/the-interpreter/debate/india-in-a-world-adrift**

LOWY INSTITUTE

India in a World Adrift

A LOWY INSTITUTE PAPER

SHIVSHANKAR MENON

PENGUIN BOOKS

UK | USA | Canada | Ireland | Australia
India | New Zealand | South Africa | China

Penguin Books is part of the Penguin Random House group of companies whose addresses can be found at global.penguinrandomhouse.com

First published by Penguin Books, 2025

Cover image by Indranil Mukherjee/AFP via Getty Images
Typeset by Midland Typesetters, Australia

Printed and bound in Australia by Griffin Press, an accredited ISO AS/NZS 14001 Environmental Management Systems printer

A catalogue record for this book is available from the National Library of Australia

ISBN 978 1 76134 900 3

penguin.com.au

We at Penguin Random House Australia acknowledge that Aboriginal and Torres Strait Islander peoples are the first storytellers and Traditional Custodians of the land on which we live and work. We honour Aboriginal and Torres Strait Islander peoples' continuous connection to Country, waters, skies and communities. We celebrate Aboriginal and Torres Strait Islander stories, traditions and living cultures; and we pay our respects to Elders past and present.

CONTENTS

CHAPTER ONE

A world between orders

Asian geopolitics do not present a pretty picture, yet the post-Cold War peace has held, prosperity has spread, and there are opportunities even in today's confusions.

In the five centuries after Vasco da Gama came to Kozhikode on the Malabar coast in 1498, European powers imposed their order on the world, relying on their dominance of the sea. The last in the line of dominant powers was the United States, which, after defeating Japan and Germany in the Second World War, established primacy over both the Atlantic, the centre of gravity in world politics at the time, and the Pacific. In those five centuries, countries and nations across the world were homogenised into the European 'Westphalian' state system of sovereign nation-states.

That era is now over in several fundamental respects. Western control of Asia's maritime spaces and dominance of the Eurasian landmass, and the superiority of Western economic and political models, are being credibly challenged. They are being challenged by continental powers, first Russia and then China, which have also sought to become maritime powers. Globalisation, technology, the consequences of the 2008 financial crisis, and the resulting course of domestic politics have combined to shake the geopolitical certainties of the last two centuries. If the First World War was primarily a European war, the Second World War a European war fought also in Asia, and the Cold War truly global, then today, the centre of gravity of world politics and the global economy is Asia. It is the possibility of conflict in Asia that concerns us for its global impact.

We are now in a world between orders, a world adrift, as it were. This is an era of contention such as we have not seen before and which seems likely to remain contested for the foreseeable future.

The signs of a world between orders are manifold. We see great power rivalry and competition, and a shifting balance of power. This is evidenced by the pathetic international response to the Covid pandemic; by the retreat from globalisation and free trade back to industrial policy and protectionism by the very powers that initiated globalisation; by tensions in hotspots ringing China from the East China Sea through Taiwan to the India–China border; by the contention over the European security order in Ukraine; by the Israeli–Palestinian dispute; and by the faltering, absent, or ineffective responses to transnational issues such as developing country debt, climate change, and terrorism. When was the last coherent international response to a transnational challenge that produced an acceptable outcome? We have not seen one since April 2009, when the London G20 summit prevented another Great Depression and stabilised the world economy. There has not been a generally binding international agreement of any consequence on major transnational issues for decades.

In these circumstances, to speak of an international order, and to use adjectives such as 'liberal' or 'rules-based' to describe it, seems inaccurate, to say the least. In any case, the order, such as it was before the 2008 financial crisis, was never very liberal or orderly for most of the world outside the West. The killing fields of the Cold War were in Asia. Whichever way the Cold War may be described, in Asia it was neither a 'long peace' nor particularly cold. An average of more than 1200 people died in wars of one type or another in Asia every day of the Cold War. And while the primary focus and origin of the

Cold War was Europe, its emphasis shifted steadily to Asia, with the most violent and lethal confrontations occurring between the Mediterranean and the Pacific in what historian Paul Thomas Chamberlin called 'the Cold War's killing fields'. Seven in ten people killed in violent conflict between 1945 and 1990 died in rimland Asia, in the almost contiguous belt of territory from the Manchurian Plain, through Korea, Indochina, and west across Central and West Asia. Here, along Asia's southern rim, more than 14 million people were killed in warfare. The Cold War also solidified the partitions of India, Korea, Palestine, Indochina, and Germany, often by local wars.

The post-Cold War era is paradoxical. We see an upsurge in deaths by conflict and forced displacement of people around the world, including in Europe, while increasing numbers of people live longer, healthier, more prosperous lives than ever before in human history.[1] We see around us a world where major powers disagree on the rules of the system, and on their hierarchy. What keeps us going is the limited agreement among major powers on what one of America's most influential Asia diplomats, Kurt Campbell, calls an 'operating system', a few general rules of the road that the great powers respect, such as the peaceful settlement of disputes and freedom of the high seas. For Campbell, these rules would include liberal values. To an outsider, it would seem that the great powers respect these values so long as there is little or no cost to themselves. For example, the South China Sea has been kept open for international shipping so far despite overlapping claims of sovereignty, and India and China have successfully de-escalated after each border crisis. It is this operating system that enabled the rise of China and other Asian powers during the globalisation decades. But the absence of an agreed global order since 2008 – the year of the global financial crisis, which marks the general, and particularly Chinese, disillusionment with US hegemony and management of the order – has resulted in increased rivalry among the great powers.

The great Australian scholar Hedley Bull once described international society as 'a group of states . . . which do not merely form a system, in the sense that the behaviour of each is a necessary factor in the calculation of the others, but also have established by dialogue and consent common rules and institutions for the conduct of their relations, and recognise their common interest in maintaining these arrangements.' Bull identified five key institutions in contemporary international society: the balance of power, international law, diplomacy, war, and great power management. These institutions help maintain and uphold a world order, which he defines as a 'pattern of activity that sustains the elementary or primary goals of the society of states, or international society'.[2] Today, we fall considerably short of forming one global international society or even a lesser form of world order.

Indeed, world order is a historical anomaly, born of a concentration of power in the hands of one nation or a group of powers, as occurred in the 13th century under the Mongols, the 19th century under European powers, and in the 20th century under the United States. For most of history, the world has consisted of multiple local orders, or multiverses, each with its own norms and views of sovereignty, boundaries, citizenship, loyalty, and the nature and role of the state and its dealings with other states. In other words, our historical experience, especially outside Europe, is of living in multiverses. It is only since the Second World War that the entire world came to consist of states defined in the Westphalian or European sense, with absolute sovereignty, hard borders, and a claim to the ultimate loyalty of the citizen, or the world of nation-states we know today.

Competition among major powers is inherent to an international system of sovereign states. It has always been so in history. Some of us may have been lulled by the fact that competition was muted for about 20 years after the end of the Cold War in 1989 by overwhelming US predominance, but this was a relatively short period. Most of the 20th century saw fierce contestation in the international order. We are now back to a more normal time of contested order. The rise of China and others in Asia has naturally provoked pushback by established powers. The main competition is between the United States and China (with Russia as a junior partner of China), and is centred on maritime Asia. It involves diplomatic, military, and economic manoeuvring between them and a struggle for the minds of everyone else. Like previous rounds of such rivalry, we see a concomitant rise in nationalism among middle and great powers.

Is this world multipolar? Governments like to say it is. It flatters them to think that they are, or will be, a pole of the world order. But this too is misleading. What I see is a world that is multipolar economically (as a result of globalisation) but unipolar militarily (though this is challenged in some regions). Politically, the world is neither multipolar nor bipolar; rather, it is confused and fragmenting.

We see three big economic blocs or areas of activity: the United States–Mexico–Canada Agreement trade area, the European Union, and the China-centred Regional Comprehensive Economic Partnership (RCEP) in Asia. But at the same time, only one power can project military force where it will, when it will, across the globe, and that is the United States. And politics is increasingly local, populist, and authoritarian, with domestic political considerations driving foreign policy decisions to an extent not often seen before. So, while the world economy remains globalised despite the best efforts of some leaders, politics has fragmented the world order. The pillars of the post-Second World War order are crumbling: the non-proliferation regime is struggling to cope with nuclear programs in Northeast Asia and the Middle East; the Bretton Woods institutions are less relevant to the world economy and developing countries; and the World Trade Organization and the multilateral system based on the United Nations is increasingly ineffective.

We tend to look to the past to understand the present, and the Cold War offers an analogy often invoked by Western commentators, perhaps because it is a comforting one as it is a war the West won. But we are not in a new Cold War today, and we would make serious policy and analytical errors were we to proceed on that assumption. This is not a world riven into two blocs, or one where democracies and autocracies are pitted against each other. The Cold War was different from our present situation in fundamental ways.

There are no two competing ideologies between China and the United States, or Russia and the United States, for that matter. Russia behaves as 19th-century European powers did, using the same tropes and narratives for justification, while China squeezes a Western ideology, Marxism, to suit its situation, with the added twist of modern technology. These powers do not manage their economies on antithetical lines while maintaining a separation from each other, as the Eastern and Western blocs did in the Cold War. All of them are part of the same global capitalist market economy created and dominated by the West, and live and die by its rules.

Nor do they offer competing political norms and models, though their internal politics differ markedly. Today, unlike the Cold War, neither China nor the United States offers an attractive model of ordering society and politics. Unlike the Soviet Union, China after Mao does not propose an alternative model of governance for the world. Indeed, China's exceptionalism creates uncertainty about whether other countries can follow its model, for China's modern rulers claim their country represents 'socialism with Chinese characteristics' rather than the 'proletarian internationalism' that Mao espoused. China appears to be a unique product of more than a century of civil war and wars on its periphery, resulting in a distinctive combination of Chinese exceptionalism and internal ordering. China's example of society and technology in the service of the overwhelming power of the party-state may be attractive to putative authoritarians, but not to their people.

Nor does the United States offer solutions. America's internal dysfunction today looks different from previous rounds, in that political populism and polarisation have made isolationism attractive across the political spectrum, and returned America to industrial policy and protectionist tools to manage its economic dealings with the world. The reliance on economic nationalism is matched by an unwillingness to subject the United States to international rules and restraints.

In some respects, the United States and China seem closer than before in their trade, industrial policy, and other choices. Foreign policy in the two greatest powers of our times is increasingly driven by internal compulsions, thus making it more transactional, and less and less relevant to others' concerns and the growing transnational problems thrown up by a globalised world.

There are no two camps for the world to formally join, which is why US partners in Asia and Europe are also part of China's Belt and Road Initiative (Beijing's signature foreign policy initiative promoting connectivity with China through the building of infrastructure on favourable terms), and seek to join the group of developing countries known as BRICS (Brazil, Russia, India, China, South Africa) while simultaneously tightening security and other links with the United States. Differences on fundamental issues, such as dealing with China and regulating the world economy strain the transatlantic alliance. The Global South – a loosely defined and loosely aligned group of developing nations in Africa, Latin America, the Caribbean, Asia, and Oceania – has yet to find alternatives to its dependence on the economic system led by the West. At the same time, China–US rivalry in Asia means that emerging powers such as Australia and India find themselves with geopolitical space, so they tighten relations with the United States because they fear the use of that space by their adversaries. They also hedge by increasing defence, security, and intelligence cooperation among themselves.

Some Chinese scholars, much like their Western counterparts, are wont to say that this is a bipolar world, for the wish is often the father of the thought. But this is clearly not the bipolar world of the 1960s and 70s. China and the United States are mutually dependent economically and part of the same globalised economic system centred on the West. Therefore, there are limits to the promised 'decoupling' of these two giant economies. Whether and how far interdependence limits their strategic rivalry is moot. But in any case, the balance of power between them remains in America's favour in most significant respects. That is why China, for all its unhappiness with the West and declarations of friendship with Russia since Moscow's 2022 invasion of Ukraine, seeks to create the impression that it respects the letter of Western sanctions on Russia and does not retaliate in kind to US sanctions on its economy and citizens.

All in all, we are in the midst of a recalibration of geopolitics and the global economy, marked by great power competition, with no clear end or victor in sight. Asia has risen, but has yet to find its equilibrium both in the world and within itself. Asia's economic fundamentals are strong, but whether it continues to rise depends on how it handles its geopolitics and its domestic politics.

The task is complicated by the fact that this round of great power rivalry is distinguished from previous ones in three fundamental ways. First, by technology, which has redefined and redistributed power among and within states, making power intangible and accessible to both states and non-state actors. Power is no longer measured solely by metrics such as GDP and military force available to the state. Trade wars and geopolitical competition are now tech wars, too. Ubiquitous information technology has changed the nature of war and made state sovereignty porous, as we see in election interference and cyber threats. The second factor is the globalised economy we are all part of, and the dependencies it creates. As countries such as China and India have accumulated power, they have become more integrated with, and therefore more dependent on, the world economy. More than half of India's GDP today consists of the external sector (broadly defined as comprising imports, exports, and international capital flows) compared to about one-fifth when radical economic reform began in 1991. Great powers, therefore, have much more incentive to engage seriously in the world and to shape the international environment. Indeed, geopolitics now becomes critical to their survival and success. Third, the new domains for contestation – cyber, outer space, and the deep ocean – add new dimensions to the security calculus of all states.

The closest historical analogy to today's great power rivalry in a globalised world may be late-19th and early-20th-century Europe, when multiple European powers at different levels of development contended for mastery and saw threats everywhere. Despite some signs of economic competition, China–US contention is primarily strategic, for power and influence, while they remain economically intertwined, as Germany and Britain were in 1914. That did not end well. Like then, ideological differences between the United States and China are not so stark as in the Cold War between the United States and the Soviet Union; both the United States and China rely on markets for economic growth, claim to be model democracies, and profess to believe that they represent the future.

However, ideological differences are sharpening as Chinese President Xi Jinping now speaks openly of the China model of development. Xi is quoted by the Chinese press as saying that 'China has debunked "the myth that modernisation means Westernisation" and hailed the Chinese model as a "paradigm for developing countries to follow"'.[3] China does not offer an alternate system of governance for the world. What it does offer is a model of development from which others can learn, though even that is qualified as being 'with Chinese characteristics' and thus less universal in its application.

Speaking on 6 March 2023, Xi Jinping said: 'Western countries headed by the United States have implemented containment from all directions, encirclement and suppression against us, which has brought unprecedented severe challenges to our country's development.'[4]

The present situation heightens geopolitical risk for the entire international system. Globalisation and technology have made the world one battlespace. In a globalised world characterised by great power rivalry, politics are in command of economics. Western sanctions on Russia are an economic price paid primarily by Europe and the Global South for the political goal of isolating and weakening Vladimir Putin's Russia. US restrictions on chip and semiconductor trade and transfers to China are politically driven.

The transition in domestic politics around the world compounds the effects of shifting balances of power, of a slowing world economy, and of limited capacity in the international system to deal with challenges. Over the last decade or so, we have seen the rise to power of new authoritarian leaders, first in large developing and emerging countries and then in advanced economies as well. Politics has turned to the right in Europe and the United States. The new authoritarians ride a rising tide of nationalism, fuelled both by fear that globalisation threatens local identities and jobs, and by the politics of distraction now that a slowing world economy makes economic and social outcomes harder to produce. Their use of nationalism and even xenophobia makes much more difficult the normal business of diplomacy, the give-and-take that negotiation and peaceful resolution of issues require. This makes geopolitical risk harder to manage successfully. The turn inwards has been accentuated by the diminution of all the powers and their leaders by the Covid pandemic and its effects. Technology, which promised freedom in the 1990s, now strengthens the trend towards authoritarian politics and state intrusion.

The shift in domestic politics, evident from the United States to China and others in between, has made all turn inwards and made us all revisionists and atavists. 'Make America Great Again', 'Build Back Better', 'China's Rejuvenation', 'Taking Centre Stage', and other such slogans, popular at home, hark back to an often mythical time and indicate a deep unease with and distrust of the world, extending to a sense of victimhood, even among those who built and benefited from the post-Second World War international order. This sense of grievance and threatened identity furthers the militarisation of policy in major powers, led by the United States and China, that we have seen in the last few years. As Xi Jinping has made clear in several ways, security, broadly defined, is now a paramount consideration in the Chinese calculus. The 'small yard, high fence' policies of the Biden administration that restricted foreign access to key technologies were also driven by security concerns rather than economic logic.

ASIA TODAY: INTEGRATION AND FRAGMENTATION

Within this global order in transition, the geopolitical situation in Asia has its own particularities.

Globally, power is now more evenly distributed across geographies than it has been for more than two centuries. While the United States and Soviet Union accounted for more than 60 per cent of world GDP and a greater proportion of military power at the height of the Cold War in 1960, China and the United States together account for less than half of world GDP and a slightly higher proportion of world military power today. Although there is only one global superpower, economic and military power is more evenly distributed, resulting in the superpower being challenged regionally.

In Asia, though no country has failed to gain from globalisation, relative economic power is now more concentrated than 30 years ago. By 2014, India and China together accounted for about half of Asia's GDP.[5] Measured by purchasing power parity (PPP: which compares the same basket of goods), they are the world's largest and third-largest economies. Most of this, of course, is accounted for by China. China is a manufacturing and trading superpower, determines commodity markets and prices globally, and accounted for about 30 per cent of global GDP growth in the decade before the pandemic. China and India's combined share of world GDP in 2023, of 21.2 per cent in nominal terms or 28.5 per cent in PPP terms, is still well below their 37.5 per cent share of world population but represents a significant economic force.[6] The shift in the overall location of economic activity is apparent in the fact that of the world's total nominal GDP of US$104.47 trillion in 2023, Asia accounted for 47.7 per cent, North America for 19.1 per cent, and Europe for 20.7 per cent.[7]

The Indo-Pacific is the most heavily militarised, including nuclearised, part of the world today. Over the last three decades, Asia's reaction to growing geopolitical uncertainty has included the rapid accumulation of weaponry, led by China. We have also witnessed the creation of a belt of nations either with nuclear weapons or edging towards them that stretches across Asia from the Mediterranean to the Pacific, from Israel to North Korea. The kindling for conflict has been collected, and the sparks to light it are available in disputes and security dilemmas across Asia from the Senkaku/Diaoyu islands through Taiwan, the South China Sea, the India–China border, and the Red Sea.

Unlike Europe, it is some time since there was an identifiable settled security order in Asia, though after Russia invaded Ukraine in 2014 and again in 2022, Europe may now be said to have joined Asia in this regard. The absence of a working Asian security architecture, institutions, or crisis management mechanisms, despite the alphabet soup of consultative and dialogue forums that meet every year, makes the situation in Asia more worrying. Still worse, those few elements of order that are intact are breaking down. North Korea's nuclear weapons and developments in the Iranian nuclear program have probably given others, including South Korea and Saudi Arabia, ideas, and risk setting off a chain reaction. China has integrated Hong Kong into its security structures despite Beijing's commitment to maintain 'one country, two systems', and Russia annexed Crimea in 2014. These successes may have taught them and others the wrong lessons about the benefits that come from unchecked territorial aggrandisement. An additional risk in Asia is that some might believe Russian propaganda that Moscow's nuclear weapons threats deterred the United States and NATO from intervening directly in Ukraine, and limited Western support for it. They may conclude that the situation is opportune for them to pursue ambitions to take territory they believe is theirs, and pursue their own agendas without fear of significant international consequences.

There is a disjuncture at the heart of Asia's geopolitics. We are more connected to each other and the rest of the world economically than ever before, but simultaneously Asia is fragmenting geopolitically.

China is the most evident example of the disjuncture, and of the frustrations it can cause. China is more powerful than it has ever been in history, yet it is more dependent on the rest of the world than ever – for food, energy, technology, commodities, and the markets essential to keeping its economy going. China's politics drive it inwards, away from the world. The Chinese government's declared 'dual circulation' policy is designed to lessen China's dependence on the world and increase the world's dependence on China. China is not unique in this. The globalised economy is also pulling India in directions its domestic politics resist. And increasingly, politics determines economic decisions.

The security of supply chains and the risk of their disruption for political reasons must now be factored into business decisions, which during the globalisation decades of the 1990s and 2000s were based purely on commercial considerations.

What, then, has kept the peace and enabled Asia's steady march to prosperity in the last three decades despite the gloomy picture painted so far? I would point to the balance of power, the balance of terror across this heavily nuclearised continent, and the operating system mentioned earlier.

The balance of power is not some natural outcome of politics, but had to be created and worked upon by the United States and others. There is no 'invisible hand' in geopolitics. So far, the major powers have worked and adjusted the balance successfully from their point of view. America's 'hub-and-spokes' alliance arrangements, centred on US predominance and presence, have by-and-large kept the peace in maritime Asia since the Vietnam War. These arrangements are now buttressed by a series of initiatives recognising and accommodating the shifting balance of power: a strengthened set of bilateral security arrangements between the United States and Japan, South Korea, Australia, and the Philippines; growing security partnerships with India and in Southeast Asia; and plurilateral formations such as the Quad (a diplomatic partnership between Australia, India, Japan, and the United States now featuring annual leaders' meetings) and AUKUS (an Australia–UK–US initiative to supply Australia with nuclear-powered submarines and cooperate on emerging military technologies) compensating somewhat for insecurities caused by the rise of China.

The United States is central to the security calculus of all of maritime Asia, yet a ring of maritime Asian states from Japan to India also hedge against diminished US interest and the unpredictability of US domestic politics by strengthening defence, security, and intelligence cooperation among themselves. The response to Washington's 2017 decision to walk out of the Trans-Pacific Partnership, a multilateral free trade agreement it initiated, has been for the Asian countries to form a successor, the Comprehensive and Progressive Agreement for Trans-Pacific Partnership. Indeed, the depth of defence, security, and intelligence ties among these countries, and the emergence of Japan in this field, has been one of the most remarkable developments of the last decade-and-a-half in Asia.

Asia's geopolitical flux makes sub-regional balances particularly important. Now that the centre of gravity of the world economy and politics is in Asia, South Asia and the Indian Ocean region have developed a significance they did not have in the Cold War, when the centre of contention was in Europe. The balance is also shifting in continental Asia as China promotes connectivity via its Belt and Road Initiative and takes a much more active political role, offering security solutions and to mediate in conflicts in South and Central Asia. In continental

Asia, China is pushing at an open door, with Russian acquiescence, unlike the pushback it faces in maritime Asia.

For most of recorded history, Asia operated in distinct multiverses – a Sinosphere in East Asia around China, an Indian Ocean world centred on India, and a complex balance among regional powers in West Asia between Egypt, Persia, Syria, and sometimes Rome and Turkey. These multiverses were in touch with each other, exchanging goods, ideas, technology, religions, and some people, but they were not part of each other's security or political calculus.

We are no longer in an Asia composed of multiverses. Now, thanks to technology and the globalisation it has enabled, each nation is intrinsic to others' security and political calculus. Local conflicts such as Ukraine have global political effects. Local geopolitical contention in Asia – in the seas near China, in Northeast Asia, in the Indian Ocean region, in West Asia, and in maritime Asia where the centre of gravity of the world's geopolitics has followed its economics – has global effects.

In the foreseeable future, Asia will likely not be centred on or dominated by a single power, but will instead be fragmented and disorderly, with Asian states hedging against all possibilities and working with China, the United States, and other powers where and when it suits them. In other words, we will see contention between powers of different strengths and attributes, and hence the formation of multiple overlapping coalitions seeking equilibrium in regional and sub-regional balances of power.

In Asia, I do not believe that history's arc is bending towards democracy as the West defines it and expects. Nor do I believe that the 'East is Rising and the West Declining', as China professes. Judging by their recent actions, neither the Chinese party-state nor the US establishment is certain that history is on their side. However, while both seek to convince others to accept that their version of the future is inevitable, Asia goes through geopolitical flux that opens space and opportunity for powers such as Australia and India. A flatter distribution of power and great power rivalry mean that middle powers are sought as partners in their regions and can play an independent role. West Asia now sees new initiatives by a host of local powers such as Israel, Saudi Arabia, Iran, and Turkey. Both Israel and Turkey attempted to mediate in 2022 when Russia invaded Ukraine again. Saudi Arabia has been in active discussions with Israel and Iran simultaneously to rework its relationships with these two antagonistic regional powers. There are balancing, hedging, and other options for independent action today that did not exist during the Cold War or the early post-Cold War period when China and the United States worked closely together in Asia. International relations theory may tell you that there is a choice to be made between balancing, hedging, and bandwagoning, but in practice some countries in Asia seem to be doing all three at the same time.

While Russia's invasion of Ukraine may have consolidated the Western alliance, it has left the rest of the world increasingly unaligned. If anything, the experience of the last decade has alienated the Global South from the traditional power centres and marginalised it at the same time. Seeing the world through the prism of China–US rivalry does not speak to the political, economic, or security interests of many Asian developing countries and undermines their commitment to international solutions to their issues. This is partly because domestic politics in the Global South are complex and autonomous, and do not align neatly with great power priorities. Concurrently, their worsening economic prospects in a slowing world economy, the hit from the Covid pandemic, and their mounting debt crises have marginalised their role and agency in the global economy.

A world between orders is thus one of increased risk and uncertainty, but also of opportunity for those with the capability. In a fragmented and uncertain order, the means and methods to cope will also be ad hoc and tentative or impermanent. This is not an era of alliances, but of issue-based coalitions of the willing and able.

A WAY FORWARD

All policy is a bet on the future. How does one plan for the future in times of heightened uncertainty such as these? None of us can predict with any certainty, though many states have tried. Tibet had a state oracle, Nechung, who told the cabinet and Dalai Lama what was coming. Earlier Indian states had astrologers. More recent 'scientific' efforts at forecasting did not prevent policy disasters, and in fact created some.

To my mind, the logical way forward is to use present trends that we consider significant to build scenarios for the future, ascribing probabilities to the likelihood of their becoming reality, and planning accordingly. Those probabilities and plans will change over time, and must be reviewed regularly if plans based on those scenarios and probabilities are to be of any use in the real world.

Let us first consider the trends in the Asian situation today that are likely to significantly impact our future. Thereafter, we will see whether these enable us to build realistic scenarios with a significant probability of coming true.

CHAPTER TWO

Global trends, Asian reverberations

The global trends considered above have strong reverberations in Asia, and indeed the most important one, China–US contention, originates in Asia. It is to the factors causing geopolitical flux in Asia that we now turn.

CHINA–US CONTENTION

The primary geopolitical fault line in Asia today is that between China and the United States. As we have seen, today's China–US rivalry is not another Cold War, as Beijing and Washington are too interlinked and interdependent economically. Decoupling and de-risking, though much spoken of, have been limited to strategically significant high-technology sectors, and have not prevented trade from growing. De-risking steps such as tariffs and sanctions have mostly been initiated by the more powerful of the two, the United States, which feels threatened by the rise of the challenger, China. This is because China still needs access to the United States along with world markets, technology, and commodities, more than the United States needs China.

The political problem, however, is a conviction on both sides that the other is determined to act against its interests. China's leadership appears convinced that the United States will oppose, contain, and restrict China's rise. The Chinese Communist Party's 20th National Congress in October 2022 confirmed that China and Xi Jinping have concluded without doubt that the United States is determined to prevent China achieving its 'rejuvenation', taking centre stage, and becoming the most advanced country in the world by mid-century. In the United States, there is bipartisan consensus that China is unfairly challenging and undercutting US pre-eminence. These convictions are compounded by the fact that both think the other has peaked, while suspecting that they themselves may have peaked too and are therefore incentivised to try to push for outcomes now.

China–US economic interdependence is now matched by the symbiotic relationship between their negative narratives about the other. The mutual escalation of opposing narratives has led the United States and China to believe their own myths about the other and made it an article of faith in each capital that the other is determined to undermine and contain them. This may become a self-fulfilling prophecy. Animosity, like ambition, once revealed cannot be recalled or undone credibly without a fundamental shift in the balance of power or overall situation. And that has not happened yet.

Politics is in command in both the United States and China: rhetoric on both sides suggests there will not be any dramatic breakthrough or easing of rivalry. Yet in the closing years of the Biden administration, mutual dependency and the potential costs of conflict led them to resume communications and attempt to create 'guardrails' for the relationship – an effort to set limits and rules for their competition. The prospect is therefore not necessarily for a worsening of the relationship. Neither wishes to be embarrassed and both will be cautious, as demonstrated by the angry but ultimately peacefully concluded incident concerning a Chinese balloon that overflew US territory, and by the visits to Beijing of US Secretary of State Antony Blinken in April 2024 followed by National Security Adviser Jake Sullivan in August. Still, domestic politics in the United States and China, rather than economic logic or shared global interests such as averting dangerous climate change, will increasingly constrain and determine the relationship.

The irony is that US economic policy is actually converging with that of China. If we examine their internal economic policies, the United States and China look more alike. The United States now has an industrial policy, is undertaking a major government-led infrastructure buildout, and is following increasingly mercantilist trade policies. China, meanwhile, is applying anti-trust rules to its big tech companies and insisting on competition, is opening up financial markets, and is seeking domestic consumption-led growth. This is not to say they are following identical policies or that they are even similar – China is still far from a market economy and the role of the state in its economy and society far exceeds anything in the United States. On international trade, we are witnessing a role reversal, since China seems keener than the United States to see the World Trade Organization restored to some effectiveness so that it can protect an open world trading system, and it is China that seeks free trade agreements such as the RCEP. There is no prospect of a US return to the Trans-Pacific Partnership, the pan-Asian trade initiative abandoned by Donald Trump, or of making the World Trade Organization effective.

The line between politics and economics is harder to draw than ever. China has weaponised – or treats as domains of contention – everything from biology to economic interdependence to its diaspora. While the United States is trying to decouple from China in technology, China is trying to create alternatives to its dependence on the United States in finance, which Beijing regards as a significant source of US global power. The Chinese have tried for years to develop indigenous technology in areas such as microprocessors, aerospace, renewable energy, and electric vehicles, with mixed success.

China–US competition is now a structural feature of global politics and is much more complex than the binary Cold War contest. It does not present clear choices and is unlikely to end in a clear denouement. Not only can there not be a clean decoupling, in areas such as semiconductors, strategically important resources (e.g. oil, gas, rare earth minerals), and renewable energy, it is hard to see decoupling without pain for both.

Interestingly, no other power is following either the US or Chinese line entirely on how to deal with the other – not Pakistan or even allies such as the Europeans. This reflects both the agency that China–US contention grants others, and also the fact that today's geopolitics, unlike the Cold War, does not offer clear binary choices. Besides, both China and the United States are increasingly domestically focused and unwilling to commit to external entanglements.

Does China's challenge mean that US hegemony is ending? Not necessarily, judging by Chinese behaviour and the limits on their competition. US policy since the Second World War has successfully prevented the emergence of a lasting peer competitor – first Germany, then Japan and Germany, and then the Soviet Union. China's challenge is more difficult. It is economically far larger than those earlier rivals, and it seeks a return to an imagined past when China was the centre of the world. Yet China remains more dependent on the United States than the other way around. While China is an economic superpower, only the United States is a global military and political power, capable of projecting military force around the world where and when it wishes. The wars in Ukraine and West Asia have shown the limitations of China's political and military power and reach. China is forced to deny selling military parts and equipment to Russia because it has to avoid being caught circumventing Western sanctions. Access to Western markets is clearly more important to China than economic ties with Russia. Hence the lack of reciprocity in the actions the United States and China are taking, with the initiative to decouple coming mostly from the United States.

Security competition between the United States and China is primarily playing out on China's maritime periphery, which has become increasingly militarised over the last two decades. Whether it is the South China Sea, Taiwan, or the Senkaku/Diaoyu islands, such tensions have traditionally been seen by China as linked to regime stability. With its economic performance no longer as strong or unquestioned as in earlier decades, China increasingly bases its legitimacy on appeals to nationalism and history. As the Chinese saying goes, 'internal disorder and external calamity' (*neiluan waihuan*) come together. The holistic definition of China's security – *zongti guojia anquanguan*; the comprehensive national security concept – which Xi Jinping tasked China's National Security Commission to achieve in November 2013 makes this clear.[8]

CHINA'S TRAJECTORY

The party-state in China has a history of great successes and great failures, and of considerable policy swings. One has only to think of China's remarkable economic achievements, which have all but eradicated extreme poverty, but also of Mao's Great Leap Forward and Cultural Revolution, the one-child policy, zero Covid, wolf warrior diplomacy, and overcommitment to the Belt and Road Initiative to see the wide range of possibilities suggested by China's recent past.

China's dilemma is that economic power based on interdependence is a double-edged sword, for it has made China dependent on the world for technology, commodities, energy, food, market access, and so on, to a level never known in China's history. China was weak and dependent under the Song, weak and independent under the Han, powerful and independent in the Qing, but never as powerful and dependent as under Xi.

China's response is to attempt a double transition: becoming a maritime power so that it can dominate the maritime spaces critical to its prosperity; and reducing its economic dependency on the outside world. The former goal may be the more difficult to attain. China's crowded geography, so unlike that of the United States, offers Beijing limited choices on its periphery and complicates its ability to project naval power. China is constrained by the so-called 'first island chain' from South Korea through to Japan and then Taiwan and the Philippines, all allies of the United States. China is also constrained by territorial disputes with other claimants in its near seas, some allied to the United States, and by the presence of significant regional military powers (Japan, South Korea, Vietnam, India) on its periphery.

If controlling its maritime periphery possibly sounds over-ambitious for China, then reducing its economic dependence on the world would require a fundamental reordering of the Chinese economy. To some extent, this has been done already. A decade ago, half of China's manufactured goods were produced through processing trade, which involves importing components and then exporting the finished goods. Today, this is less than 20 per cent, with 70 per cent of exported goods produced domestically.

The Chinese Communist Party knows what needs to be done for the economy, and agreed a major reform program at the third plenum of the Central Committee in 2013. But vested interests and politics (and, more recently, post-Covid economic headwinds) have prevented the implementation of many of the structural elements of that program. Instead, the Party has carried out some necessary reforms in environmental protection, the one-child policy, healthcare, interest rate liberalisation, and the opening of the financial sector. But harder jobs remain, such as land reform, reform of the *hukou* system that regulates internal migration, taxation, privatisation, and labour practices.

China's domestic economic situation has limited the scale and nature of China's post-Covid economic recovery. The property crisis and skyrocketing debt levels are major impediments and resemble what Japan faced 20 years ago, though South Korea at the turn of the century may be a more apt comparison in terms of development and income levels. Deflating the property bubble has proved hard. Chinese local governments face impossible demands: to stimulate growth and cut debt at the same time. Structural issues, too, are serious. China's working-age population peaked in 2015, and growth in total factor productivity has declined since 2011, reflecting the fact that much of China's economic activity now takes place in low productivity state-owned enterprises.

China's economic policy dilemma is unenviable. If a Chinese recovery is to be based on domestic consumption and not on investment, as in the past, it is liable to fuel inflation abroad by pushing up energy, food, and commodity prices. If, on the other hand, the government resorts to the traditional fixes of infrastructure spending, investment in state-owned enterprises, and exports, the external protectionist backlash will be considerable. China has difficult options to choose from: rising debt, rising unemployment, or wealth transfers to households. Since the party-state cannot risk a collapse in GDP and rising unemployment, it has so far chosen to boost credit and raise debt. The present leadership's choice has been to turn increasingly statist, doubling down on industrial policy, and betting on control of advanced technologies for the future.

China has entered an adjustment period, as did previous East Asian miracle economies – Japan, South Korea, and Taiwan – after a 30–40-year growth spurt. In each case, the adjustment was more difficult than expected, provoking a reworking of the social and political contract. It brought democracy to Taiwan and South Korea, and led Japan's Liberal Democratic Party to lose its monopoly on power for a while. Democracy seems most unlikely in China, but that does not mean we are not seeing a reworking of the political and social contract. Today, the Communist Party under Xi Jinping is building a hard security state to maintain social stability, control political life, and avoid the fate of the Communist Party of the Soviet Union. China stopped publishing data on 'mass incidents' (protests involving more than 100 people) when they passed 200,000 per year in 2013. In response to internal stresses, China now spends more on internal security than on its military. The party-state has built an unprecedented surveillance apparatus, further tightened in the pandemic, to provide early warning and control society. Surveillance technologies and data integration tools have been exported by China to at least 80 countries as of 2019.

Xi Jinping is a strong-state ethno-nationalist, not another Mao Zedong. Mao distrusted the Party, bureaucracy, and intellectuals, believed in class struggle, and was an internationalist who sought permanent revolution at home. Xi is primarily a nationalist who is building a party-state, ideology, and institutions for China's greatness, as he sees it. Since the 20th National Congress in October 2022, Xi has doubled down on his policies: centralising power in his own hands, appointing a Politburo Standing Committee of people who have been his personal aides (thus risking the creation of an echo chamber), securitising policy at the expense of the economy, and promoting a bleak assessment of the outside world.

Since 2017, Xi increasingly uses the phrase 'changes in the world unseen in a century' to indicate a pair of ideas: that China is approaching the centre of the world stage, and that risks and difficulties become greater as the party-state nears its goal of national rejuvenation. Xi's answer, in his new security concept, is for China to be more proactive and preventive in its approach to all threats, moving away from 'stability maintenance' to 'prevention and control'. This is what India saw in its clashes with the People's Liberation Army (PLA) on its border – known as the Line of Actual Control – in Ladakh in spring 2020, when the PLA moved to pre-empt future Indian consolidation of its hold on areas it had long patrolled by moving into them before Indian infrastructure was completed.

China seeks to create an image of an all-powerful and ever-successful nation that represents the future, in opposition to a declining United States that represents the 20th century. But a country that, since 2012, spends more on internal security than on national defence cannot be assumed to be politically and socially attractive or stable. Nor should we exaggerate China's influence beyond its immediate periphery. As the Ukraine War has shown, China's power to influence political and military outcomes abroad remains limited, although Beijing has used the opportunity to consolidate Russia's dependence on China. China's global influence is economic, and its coercive use of economic tools in the last decade has displayed both the reach and the limits of that power. In several cases where Beijing has used economic leverage – against Canada, South Korea, Japan, India, and Australia – China is today less influential than before. Bear in mind also China's respect for the letter of US sanctions on Russia, and Russia's military, political, and economic absence in most of Asia and the Indo-Pacific, where China's primary interests lie. The geopolitical impact of the China–Russia alliance is primarily confined to Central Asia and the economy.

The most likely prospect is a powerful but frustrated China – hard, brittle, and touchy. The goals the Party has set for itself may not be attainable. The domestic reasons are well known: declining demography, a faltering economy, and internal stresses prompting investment in internal security and a vast domestic surveillance apparatus. Externally, it is not just pushback by the United States, other powers, and neighbours, but the nature of today's Asian geopolitics that complicates China's task. Xi's turn inwards and towards party centrality will likely continue. China will be assertive where it sees the relative balance of power being in its favour – as in the South China Sea with the Philippines, and on the border with India – will move into what it considers 'vacant spaces' such as the South Pacific, and be tactically accommodative where it is uncertain of its power, as with the United States and Japan. This is not necessarily a reassuring prospect for Asia.

THE WORLD ECONOMY

In a globalised world characterised by great power rivalry, China's economic slowdown has global consequences. China's contribution to global growth slowed dramatically after the Covid pandemic, from close to 33 per cent between 2010 and 2019 to about 21 per cent now. While China remains the most powerful growth engine in the world, its role is diminishing. Others have not yet taken up the slack. India, which was equal to one-third of China's contribution to global growth in 2010–19, is now almost doubling its contribution.[9] The US share has been a steady ten per cent or so for a long time, while Europe and the rest are less consequential. China, the United States, and India are the three sources of global economic growth likely to matter the most.

The future of globalisation is today an open question. Trade is fragmenting as countries impose barriers on the flow of goods and capital in the name of friendshoring, de-risking, or self-reliance. Around 3000 trade-restricting measures were imposed in 2023, nearly three times the number imposed in 2019. Yet global trade to GDP is now 60 per cent, and economies are much more integrated into global markets and value chains, so we are not witnessing de-globalisation but a reordering of the globalised economy. The share of trade to global GDP has stayed relatively stable since 2011, fluctuating between 55 per cent and 60 per cent. Trade and GDP growth have both slowed, and foreign direct investment is segmenting along geopolitical lines.[10] According to the UN Conference on Trade and Development, 2023 global foreign direct investment flows of US$1.37 trillion were weak and mostly to developed economies, a decline of 18 per cent over the previous year.

The probability of the world economy fragmenting into large regional trading blocs is higher than ever before. With the declining effectiveness of the World Trade Organization and rise of protectionism in major trading economies, a higher proportion of trade is taking place within the three large trading blocs – the United States–Mexico–Canada Agreement trade area in North America, the European Union, and the China-centred RCEP in Asia.

Great power rivalry poses further risks to the world economy. For instance, it has raised the risk of financial de-globalisation as countries react to the expropriation of Russian reserves and Russia being frozen out of the SWIFT international payments system after its invasion of Ukraine. We already see Russian and Chinese attempts to rely on payment systems not linked to the US dollar and not routed through the United States, and some BRICS members have sought to move away from the US dollar as a reserve currency. If these trends continue, we should expect competing payment systems to become barriers to cross-border capital flows. But there is no alternative yet in sight for the US dollar as a store of value. China's attempts to move out of US Treasuries since 2008 have had little success, and it would take a major economic convulsion for the world to move away from the US dollar as its preferred reserve currency.

The other economic effect of great power rivalry in Asia has been a reordering of global value chains thanks to onshoring, friendshoring, and other forms of risk mitigation. This involves the relocation of manufacturing from China to countries such as Vietnam and Mexico, which have freer access to Western markets, particularly the United States. Much of this capacity is, however, created by Chinese firms and investors, and in some cases by the export of industrial plants from China; Vietnam's garment industry is a good example of this trend. There is also the creation of fresh alternative capacity outside China to build resilience, in case it becomes more difficult for companies to manufacture inside China, in what is known as the 'China plus one' strategy. Among recent examples are Apple's decision to manufacture iPhones in India and iPads in Vietnam. Interestingly, the net effect over the last decade of such decoupling or de-risking efforts is that although global value chains in manufacturing have been shrinking, those in services are growing, thus creating opportunities for countries with skills in services, such as Australia and India.

WORLD ORDER

I have argued that we are now in a world between orders. It is multipolar economically, unipolar militarily, and confused and local politically. National politics is producing new authoritarians who depend on an outsize image and hyper-nationalism for legitimacy, making our period of great power rivalry more dangerous and uncertain.

As a consequence, multilateralism as we knew it is dead. There has not been a binding international agreement on an issue of consequence for more than a decade-and-a-half. When states quarrel among themselves, how can organisations formed and led by them be effective? Organisations composed of member states, such as the United Nations and its specialised agencies like the World Health Organization, only work when their member states want them to work. Great power rivalry means that they cannot agree to make them work, as we saw in the abject response to Covid, in the weaponisation of relief and aid in Gaza, and the poor response to the 2023 earthquake in southern Turkey. It is the international system's inability to cohere and produce outcomes that makes climate change such an outstanding challenge with serious geopolitical effects. To my mind, there is as yet no sign of effective multilateral action on transnational threats such as climate change, the militarisation of outer space, or the developing country debt crisis.

We see the consequences of the absent international order in multiple domains – in migration, in local conflicts, and in the space that middle powers and revisionists see to pursue their own agendas: Israel in Gaza, Russia in Ukraine, China in the Himalayas and South China Sea, Iran and Saudi Arabia in Yemen, and elsewhere in Congo, Sudan, Libya, even the Maldives . . . the list is long.

Since the cowardly Hamas terrorist attack on Israel on 7 October 2023, multiple actors have worked to fundamentally refashion the politics of the Middle East. Israel has displayed an ability to strike at enemies in the heart of Tehran, has eliminated Iran's air defences around significant nuclear sites, and exposed the vulnerability of Iran's military, missile, and nuclear assets, to say nothing of the Iranian leadership. This would not have been possible without US agreement at the very least, and some level of enabling support, both of which continue.

One consequence of the rapid unravelling of the Iranian position in the region and serial revelations of its weakness might well be an Iranian determination to accelerate its quest for nuclear weapons, which has been signalled and used for negotiating leverage but not pursued determinedly since 2004.

Iranian weakness also opened the door for the redrawing of the region's geopolitics via the collapse of the Assad regime in Syria in December 2024. Russia's preoccupations in Ukraine, Hezbollah's degradation by Israel, and Iran's vulnerability made it possible for a combination of insurgent and terrorist groups (such as Hayat Tahrir al-Sham, which includes groups and leaders from the former Salafi al-Nusra Front of Al-Qaeda) and the Syrian National Army to topple the Assad regime relatively peacefully. They were aided by the Turkish army and Israeli and US military actions to suppress the Assad regime's military forces.

The lessons of these changes, which tilt the regional balance in favour of Israel and the United States, cannot be lost on other local regimes and leaders, particularly Saudi Arabia and Egypt, who had moved towards more independent foreign policy stances, cultivating relations with Russia and China, both of which proved powerless to protect Assad, affect the course of events in Gaza, and prevent action against Iran.

How long the new arrangements will last is an open question, should the Trump administration prove isolationist and unwilling to underwrite them with US military presence and power, and in the face of the growing alienation between the Arab street and regimes. The risks of anarchy in Syria, of a resurgence of terrorist groups, and of ever more brutal and vicious forms of pushback, are real.

We also see the absence of international order in the plight of displaced people. According to the United Nations, between 7 October 2023 and April 2024, 1.9 million Gazans, overwhelmingly civilians, representing 85 per cent of the Strip's population, were forced by Israeli military action to flee their homes, but remain trapped in the Gaza Strip. While the primary causes of this violence are longstanding and local, the absence of an international order has enabled it to assume the proportions that it has. The humanitarian crisis and plight of the Palestinians contributes to the growing number of internally displaced persons across the globe. Amid war and conflict, climate-related disasters, and other humanitarian crises, tens of millions of people each year flee their homes to escape danger, but the majority never cross international borders. According to the Geneva-based Internal Displacement Monitoring Centre, 2022 saw a record 71.1 million internally displaced people, more than double the number in 2012.

Russia's war in Ukraine has also highlighted the fraying of the international non-proliferation regime. Moscow has made nuclear threats, leading to widespread discussion about the possible use of nuclear weapons. The invasion has exposed the ineffectiveness of the 1994 Budapest Memorandum, in which Russia, the United States, and the United Kingdom pledged to respect Ukraine's territorial integrity and sovereignty in exchange for Ukraine's accession to the Non-Proliferation Treaty and giving up the nuclear weapons on its soil. Others are likely to conclude that only the weapons themselves, not legal instruments, are effective guarantees of security.

Because the order is fragmenting, no one-size solution fits the entire range of security issues facing Asia. The focus must therefore be on issue-based coalitions of the willing and able. The success of bilateral and plurilateral arrangements such as AUKUS and I2U2, a partnership between India, Israel, the United Arab Emirates, and the United States on global challenges, is proof of that. As is the Quad, which is now working to enhance maritime security, resilience of supply chains, and providing other public goods in the Indo-Pacific. The post-Cold War peace in Asia has held through ad-hoc and occasional arrangements, allowing for rapid adjustments to a shifting balance of power. This is why there is no real support in Asia for a NATO presence or mission, or for rigid NATO-style security arrangements. The present sense of insecurity does not translate into such support. Asia's experience of 45 million killed in combat when Cold War structures were in place argues against the import of such security concepts. We have since seen 40 years of peace. Asia would seem to have done better without a rigid security architecture, instead dealing pragmatically with the issues.

THE MIDDLE POWERS AND THE GLOBAL SOUTH

So far, we have concentrated on the interactions between Asia's larger states and the geopolitical and geoeconomic risks that their interactions pose. But there are two Asias.

As globalisation enriched some, it impoverished others. With the blow of the Covid pandemic and a pathetic international response (weaker than the world managed in the face of HIV/AIDS), much of the Global South has been lost to the North politically. It now seeks another way. Developing country debt has grown to massive proportions. The International Monetary Fund estimates that more than 53 developing countries are at risk of a debt crisis. Despite repeated promises at the G20 and the multilateral development banks, most of them are yet to find adjustment packages and support to deal with their debt. Some among the South speak of facing the financial equivalent of the vaccine apartheid of Covid.

Sri Lanka is a representative case. The pandemic stopped tourism, crashed commodity prices, and reduced remittances to near zero. Foreign exchange earnings collapsed and Sri Lanka defaulted on its debt in April 2022. It took more than a year-and-a-half for the first cent of international assistance and an adjustment program to be agreed. The cause was great power rivalry. The West was unwilling to help Sri Lanka pay off China, which owned more than 20 per cent of Sri Lanka's debt. China would refinance Sri Lanka's debt but would not write off or reschedule it for fear that other countries, to which China has committed US$1 trillion in Belt and Road Initiative funding, would ask for the same. Meanwhile, the International Monetary Fund was waiting for China and other creditors to agree among themselves before it would come to Sri Lanka's aid. In the event, India helped Sri Lanka tide over that period, offering US$3.8 billion to the end of 2023, even though little of Sri Lanka's debt is to India.

Today, more than 40 countries of the Global South want to join the BRICS group of developing nations, even though it does not yet have a successful record of creating economic or political outcomes. Uncertainty leads the South to look for alternatives to existing institutions and systems. Today, BRICS includes energy superpowers such as Iran and Russia, and economic heavyweights such as China and India. In terms of trade, investment, and GDP volumes, BRICS may have caught up with the G7 with its expansion in 2023. Yet it still lacks ideological coherence or economic accomplishments other than the New Development Bank.

The rise of BRICS has diminished the ability of Western sanctions to isolate countries Washington declares 'rogue'. Despite the West's economic war against Russia, Moscow now exports as much oil and natural gas as when its full invasion of Ukraine began in 2022. That is thanks largely to a boom in trade with countries outside Europe and North America that have not imposed sanctions, most importantly China. Russia's balance of payments with China is in heavy deficit, and most of the increase in trade is in Russian imports of Chinese goods. That has caused a glut in Russian export facilities, which once facilitated trade with Europe and now sit unused. This phenomenon takes tangible form in a pile-up of empty shipping containers affecting the global logistics market.

One thing members of the Global South share is a common experience as victims of colonialism, making them allergic to self-appointed spokespersons or leaders. Besides, this is not the bipolar Cold War world that enabled the rise of the Non-Aligned Movement. In a globalised economy, with developing countries at different stages of economic modernisation, the 'Global South' includes a variety of interests. So, this is no bloc in the making. What is clear is that most of them do not want to be dragged into choosing sides in great power rivalries, and are adopting hedging or balancing strategies vis-à-vis the great powers. This was most evident recently when many of them distanced themselves from the Western stance on Ukraine at the United Nations, and was reinforced by the apparent hypocrisy revealed when, after the Hamas terrorist attack, Israel's military occupation of Gaza did not receive the same treatment by the West as Russia's invasion of Ukraine.

If we are to stabilise the situation and reduce uncertainty, the international system should be seen to be addressing the concerns of the Global South, a South that is increasingly significant not only as an arena for great power competition but as a source of growth in the world economy, and as an actor in most conflicts. I see no alternative to an effective dialogue and understanding between the developed world and Global South to deal with transnational challenges and to devise international arrangements to deal with them. We now require a new set of rules and a new architecture of global governance in which the Global South has a place and a stake. It should not take another world war to force us to do so.

UKRAINE

Should Ukraine figure in this list of things to watch? Perhaps. But to my mind, for all the noise, Ukraine is primarily a local geopolitical issue with local consequences, a fight among Europeans about the European order, except that in a globalised world it has significant second-order economic and other effects, risking a global energy crisis, a spike in world food prices, inflation, and so on. Western unity created by the Russian invasion of 2022 is already showing signs of strain, and the effectiveness of economic sanctions, which depend on universality, is increasingly doubtful. Arms supplies to Ukraine are flagging, and the Russian economy seems to be bearing the brunt of Western economic sanctions while continuing to grow. The question remains: how big an economic price is the West willing to pay for the political goal of isolating and degrading Russia?

The war in Ukraine has already distracted the United States and the West from Asia and raised questions about Western staying power in future contests. Attempts by the former Biden administration to put 'guardrails' around China–US contention through dialogue with the Chinese leadership gathered strength in part due to Western preoccupation with Ukraine and the war in Gaza. But the Ukraine War, which is a war about European order, will not determine the situation in Asia or the outcome of the contest between the United States and China.

The longer-term prospect is of a Europe preoccupied with its own order. Whoever wins this war, or even if neither side does, Europe will be unstable, with a revisionist state (the loser) unsettling it for many years. The war in Ukraine also accelerates Russia's secular decline, which in turn diminishes its capacity for independent action and increases its dependence on China. However, the Russia–China alliance should not be overestimated. It is an alliance of animus against the West, but neither side can do much for the other's primary concerns: for China these are Taiwan, the US presence in Asia, and reducing its dependence on the United States; for Russia they are NATO's steady expansion, European order, Ukraine, and its influence in its near abroad.

THE RISK OF CONFLICT

Will the unstable and uncertain situation in Asia described here result in conflict between the great powers? One way to approach this question might be to examine what has kept the peace that enabled unprecedented prosperity in Asia over three decades. Can we expect that to continue? The answers might suggest how we should look at security in Asia today.

I would attribute the peace that enabled Asia's steady march to prosperity in the last 30 years to three factors: the balance of power, the balance of terror created by nuclear weapons across this heavily nuclearised continent, and Kurt Campbell's 'operating system'. These three factors enabled the rise of China, India, and other Asian countries during the 1990s and early 21st century.

Today, both the balance of power and balance of terror are shifting rapidly, and the operating system is fraying. The signs are in the steady increase in Chinese military deployments around Taiwan, leaving us closer to crisis; in the continuing unwillingness of China and the Philippines to lower tensions in the South China Sea; and in the inability of multiple institutions to find a modus vivendi for increasingly fraught security dilemmas throughout maritime Asia. The UN Convention on the Law of the Sea proved ineffective even after the Philippines won a case before an international tribunal in 2016 about its dispute with Beijing in the South China Sea. Others have therefore not sought redress in international institutions. The fraying of the operating system has resulted in unfettered great power rivalry. On the Eurasian continent, we have recently been reminded by the terrorist attacks on Israel, and by Azerbaijan's takeover of Nagorno-Karabakh, of how fragile the situation is.

The proliferation of weapons of mass destruction in Asia is another source of instability. Given the Ukrainian and Libyan experience, the temptation for threshold nations to seek security in the possession of nuclear weapons must be strong. The spread and improvement of nuclear arsenals suggests that without credible structures of deterrence in Northeast Asia and West Asia, North Korea's nuclear capabilities could provoke similar ambitions in South Korea and, ultimately, in Japan. Since North Korea acquired nuclear weapons, a majority of South Koreans believe their country should also possess them. That would leave Japan as the only non-nuclear weapon state in Northeast Asia. Similarly, should Iran go nuclear, it could trigger ambitions in neighbours such as Saudi Arabia, Turkey, and the United Arab Emirates. In none of these cases is America's so-called extended nuclear deterrent (its nuclear umbrella) credible anymore. Why would a superpower patron risk their own populations to a nuclear counterstrike to defend an ally?

The region's prosperity and accumulation of power are also dependent on security in the maritime space. China's attempt to become a maritime power is both understandable and destabilising. Maritime Asia is the arena where China–US contention plays itself out, yet geography and security differ from one part of the Indo-Pacific to the other. The Western Pacific is an open geography dominated by the United States; the seas near China are closed and contested, and have therefore been battlespaces in history; the Indian Ocean has always been an ocean of trade and travel rather than battles, even during the 20th-century world wars. Risks, actions, and outcomes therefore differ markedly from one part of maritime Asia to the other.

China–US contention in these spaces, China's naval build-up, and the countervailing presence of other significant naval powers such as India, Japan, and Australia have so far kept the maritime peace and the sea lanes open. The United States is today more integrated into Asia's maritime security and works with many more partners than a decade ago. Instead of imitating US strategy in maritime Asia, which it would find difficult to achieve without allies, China has followed an 'insurgent' strategy that makes ports available to support PLA naval operations far from home without the drawbacks of going up directly against established powers such as the United States. It has invested commercially in ports around the region and the world (95 at last count), and the PLA Navy had called at 27 of them by the end of 2023. Beijing has also built naval bases for friendly countries such as Cambodia, Myanmar, and Bangladesh that far exceed local needs. Capacities have thus been built without the disadvantages of military alliances and the costs of public opposition. Whether and to what extent this use of economic power to achieve strategic goals will actually work is moot.

The diffusion of power in Asia also means that not all issues depend on, or can be dealt with by, China and the United States, even if they were to agree or put aside their contention, unlikely as that may seem. While the United States and China are preponderant in military and economic terms over the other powers in Asia, they are both also challenged in some theatres and domains – for instance, on the Korean Peninsula (where neither can get their way), in South Korea–Japan relations, and in Vietnam's

South China Sea policy. As China–US tensions have risen, so have military budgets throughout Asia. Between 2017 and 2022, military budgets adjusted for inflation grew by almost 60 per cent in the Philippines, more than 35 per cent in China, and around 10–15 per cent in South Korea, Pakistan, Vietnam, and Indonesia.[11]

Technology and weapons are more widely held, opening up new domains for contestation. Apart from cyber and outer space, undersea competition in Asia (involving seabed internet cables, marine resources, and underwater sensors to detect ships and submarines) is now a reality that countries such as India and Australia have to deal with.

The regional response to shifts in the balance of power has been predictable: strengthening existing alliances and partnerships to balance China while simultaneously hedging against changes in both Chinese and US policy. This is not a situation that promotes new alliances or Asia-wide security structures and architectures. There is no common threat to internal order leading to an alliance or virtual alliance (as communist insurgencies led to the formation of the Association of Southeast Asian Nations or the French Revolution led to the Concert of Europe). If anything, China is offering autocrats, dictators, and new authoritarians the tools and know-how to tighten their grip on their societies, presenting a viable alternative to alliance-building.

But more than the choice between the United States and China that other states seek to avoid making, it is the local kindling and its potential to lead to conflict that should worry us. Speaking to the UN General Assembly on 6 February 2023, UN Secretary-General António Guterres warned, 'I fear that the world is not sleepwalking into a wider war. I fear it is doing so with its eyes wide open.'[12] Great power contention and the absence of an international order do not necessarily lead to conflict. For most of history, we have not had an order, and certainly not a world order. Yet we have managed to find ways to keep the peace for extended periods. The absence of a world order need not worry us. It is the presence of disputes, and the present inability of the international system to resolve or manage them, that should worry us. That is what heightens the risk of conflict, and not only between great powers, which are unlikely to fight each other directly due to their nuclear arsenals. But as the political scientist Robert Jervis understood, this presents a paradox: 'to the extent that the military balance is stable at the level of all-out nuclear war, it will become less stable at lower levels of violence'.[13]

Consider the possible sources of conflict in Asia today.

China–United States

Who would initiate war between China and the United States? The United States, thinking that China is catching up and that it should therefore move now rather than later? Or China, knowing that it has peaked, and should maximise its gains while its relative power is at its height? Such a calculus may have appeared reasonable to some during the Cold War, but today China and the United States are joined at the hip economically, and neither can be certain of the outcome of a direct conflict. Whatever its extent, location, and scope (and it would be hard for anyone to predict or control once it started), such a conflict would do irreparable damage to both.

Taiwan

There is no assurance of victory if China chooses kinetic means to reunify Taiwan, whether slowly (by 'salami slicing' small offshore islands, using blockades, or imposing economic sanctions against Taiwanese imports to China) or quickly, by a full-scale invasion. No Chinese leader could afford to fail in this enterprise. Nor can anyone predict the outcome of a military conflict over Taiwan or be confident that the scenarios short of full-scale invasion would succeed. There is little urgency in authoritative Chinese leadership statements on Taiwan, though PLA generals and admirals are much more assertive and threatening, talking up the possibility of conflict, as are their US counterparts. Today, it is uncertainty about the outcome that keeps the peace, not a lack of desire for unification on China's part. What is worrying is the Chinese party-state's increasing coordination of military gestures with 'united front' tactics (networks and key individuals controlled or influenced by the Chinese Communist Party operating in Taiwan) to divide opinion in Taiwan, creating pretexts for interventions by China. Taiwan is an instance where, despite the interest of all sides to continue the status quo, fear of disadvantage in the future could lead to rash actions. We are not there yet, and since for the present no one can be certain of victory in conflict over Taiwan, the peace holds.

South China Sea

If there is one place where an imbalance of power among various claimants might tempt the more powerful to use force, it is in the South China Sea. We saw an escalation in tensions and actions between

China and the Philippines in 2024, but in each previous case these tensions have ultimately been dialled down. The US naval presence and the significance of the waterway to international trade, to the strategic stability of China's near seas, and to Taiwan probably account for the fact that tensions have not so far resulted in conflict. Until that equation changes fundamentally, we are likely to see a continuation of the present tensions short of direct conflict. However, the gradual escalation of Chinese actions around nearby Taiwan – threatening blockades and other forms of military action short of full-fledged conflict – is concerning for the South China Sea region.

Korean Peninsula

There can be opposing views on whether the acquisition of nuclear weapons by North Korea has increased the probability of conflict, and on whether it has destabilised the situation in Northeast Asia. It has certainly ensured that the logical response in South Korea, and ultimately Japan, will be to acquire matching capabilities, thus making all Northeast Asian countries nuclear weapons states. Could this stabilise the situation short of war? Possibly, if instead of the quixotic American quest to denuclearise the Korean Peninsula, all the countries concerned were to build a stable structure of deterrence. But the immediate risk of conflict initiated by a nuclear-armed North Korea may not be more than it was before it acquired nuclear weapons. Kim Jong Un's quest to develop nuclear weapons with the capability to hit the continental United States ensures that if he were to start military action against the South, the joint South Korean and allied response would likely hit North Korea and all its nuclear sites so thoroughly as to prevent an attack on the US mainland.

India–China

In 2020, China's military moved forward along the western sector of its disputed border with India, the so-called Line of Actual Control, causing the first deaths by hostile action there in 45 years. The PLA has since prevented Indian troops from accessing several dozen patrolling points that they visited before 2020. One explanation for what China did in 2020 is that it wanted to show India that the United States could not solve India's problem with China. Another is that it wanted to show neighbours such as Bhutan and Nepal that India cannot even take care of itself let alone their security, meaning they should therefore deal directly with China. If those were China's goals, they were not fully achieved. Given China's military advantage, the temptation for a further use of force on the Line remains. India, on the other hand, has been careful in its resort to force to settle the boundary dispute and in its responses to Chinese provocations.

Restoring deterrence on the India–China border is essential to minimise the possibility of conflict. Both governments are still to find ways to manage their disagreements on the boundary and the imbalance in military power, which has grown in recent times as China has built more military infrastructure and deployed advanced aircraft on the Line. Probably the best we can hope for in the short term is a managed rivalry. China cannot easily be defeated, nor can or should it be isolated. But the Chinese Communist Party is too ruthless to trust. Managed rivalry is a better alternative than foolish, intemperate steps that will end in war, but it requires deep historical knowledge of China and the Communist Party.

India–Pakistan

Given Pakistan's internal preoccupations and weaknesses, and its worries to the west in Afghanistan, the renewed ceasefire on the Line of Control between India and Pakistan, which has now held for more than three years, will likely endure. But India must always calculate that this could be deception and might be reversed quickly. Besides, Pakistan is a subset of India's China problem. The recent precipitous decline in India–China relations, the US withdrawal from Afghanistan, and sharper China–US friction, have all made Pakistan more useful to China – 'a strategic strong point', as the Chinese now say. The PLA and Pakistan Army now have interoperability that comes from common hardware, compatible communications, and information systems that can talk to each other. China probably seeks from Pakistan the functions often provided by an ally, such as logistical support links, basing, capability aggregation, and diversion of adversaries. The only sure guarantee of peace for India is a favourable balance of military power with Pakistan.

This brief survey suggests that increasing great power rivalry, alongside the absence of a functioning international order, has raised the risk of conflict in several flashpoints, and bears careful watching. But I would argue that the possibility of direct great power conflict in Asia is not as high as that of one of the flashpoints erupting due to miscalculation or error.

In the Cold War, the great powers were happy to let others do their fighting for them, while today, Russia and China are fighting wars directly in

Ukraine and the Himalayas. Still, given the situations in Myanmar, Central Asia, West Asia, and in the seas near China, the risk of proxy wars, civil conflict, and attacks below the threshold of conventional conflict (such as through aid to insurgents and the use of terrorist proxies) means asymmetric efforts to upend the status quo in Asia are higher than ever since the Vietnam War.

That is what logic tells us. But states and their leaders are not the purely rational actors beloved of economists and political scientists. If they were, we would all behave alike and would be able to predict each other's future actions. We should never underestimate human folly, or what the British call the 'moron risk premium'. Therefore, one cannot rule out direct conflict between the great powers. The likelihood of such conflict may not be as high as that of violence within and between smaller states. But that does not preclude mistakes, proxy wars, great power involvement in civil and other conflicts, and increasing friction in the international system. The answer in such cases is to restore or build credible structures of deterrence. Rather than seeking unattainable goals (such as the denuclearisation of the Korean Peninsula), the focus should be on putting in place agreements and confidence-building measures, for instance mutual declarations among nuclear-armed nations that none will be the first to use nuclear weapons (so-called 'no first use' pledges). It also means accepting the new reality of heightened military and nuclear preparations in Asia and working with it.

Finally, what might be done in this situation to minimise the risks and mitigate the challenges that uncertainty and great power rivalry have brought us?

Because the order is fragmenting and power is increasingly diffused, no one-size security architecture or solution fits the entire range of security issues in the Indo-Pacific and Asia. My mantra is issue-based coalitions of the willing and able. The Quad's success is proof of that. As is the success of the other plurilateral and bilateral arrangements, such as AUKUS and I2U2. Forums where all those who are ready to work with likeminded others can participate in promoting an open and inclusive set of security arrangements in maritime Asia have a higher chance of success in today's fragmented Asia than the alternatives. The last few years have seen considerable progress in some areas, such as maritime security and resilience of supply chains. But much more can and needs to be done, particularly to prepare crisis management mechanisms before crises hit us, and to address local sources of instability.

CHAPTER THREE

Scenarios

Now that we have considered some of the major factors affecting Asia's geopolitics, what do they tell us about the future? Three broad scenarios can be sketched.

BUSINESS AS USUAL

There are naturally those, particularly in the established powers, who expect or work for a perpetuation of the present balance of power, or to restore their dominance in the international system. This essentially conservative effort is to maintain the balance of economic and military power that underpinned the Western-led order after the Second World War. The benefits of the existing international system can lead them to a natural desire and expectation to continue a favourable power balance.

This expectation has been buttressed in the United States by the slowdown in the Chinese economy, the US economy's success since the 2008 financial crisis, and the consolidation of the Western alliance that Russia's invasion of Ukraine and China's rise have brought about.

To my mind, however, we can rule out business as usual scenarios. These scenarios often assume that the United States and China will manage to avoid conflict and not worsen their relationship; that the world economy will continue to grow and stay globalised; that emerging economies will continue to catch up with the developed world; that international cooperation will mitigate climate change; and that although the Chinese Communist Party will succeed in building a centralised security state with a capitalist economy and single-party rule, China and other successful emerging economies will be accommodated within existing international institutions and power structures rather than challenge US leadership.

Acting on such assumptions is likely to result in disappointment. The chances of each of these assumptions coming true are small; of all of them aligning are miniscule. Life never stands still and the future is never a straight line extrapolation from the past. We are in a time of rapid and unpredictable change, a world where all the powers are revisionist, and where economic and military power is being redefined and redistributed, not least by technological and energy revolutions. To expect more of the same at such a time, and then to do the same thing in different circumstances expecting similar results, would be a recipe for trouble.

If, based on our collective experience, we expect change, then one can build both pessimistic and optimistic scenarios.

PESSIMISTIC SCENARIOS

Pessimists would expect China–US contention to result in conflict, direct or through proxies, most likely in the seas around Taiwan or the South China Sea. These scenarios would also see China's dimming economic prospects and inability to structurally reform without affecting the Party's hold on power as leading to an increasing reliance on nationalism, with severe consequences for the global economy. The world will be divided into rival trading blocs, reversing the integration that globalisation has brought about, and resulting in military alliances and hypernationalism among the great powers. In this telling, the combination of geopolitical risk and economic slowdown leads to conflict between the great powers, as it did in the 1930s. Large multilingual states will see increased violence from separatist movements and religious and ethnic groups, enabled by technology. Climate change will be unaddressed and will soon create humanitarian disasters of epic proportions.

Some evidence for such scenarios already exists. Deaths by conflict are at an all-time high since the Second World War, as are the numbers of internally and internationally displaced persons. The militarisation of society and politics, and the securitisation of policy, are features of most great powers in this century. Global economic growth has slowed since 2008 and has yet to recover from the shock of the Covid pandemic. The main driver of the world economy before the pandemic, China, is no longer in a position to provide the same global stimulus, and it will take time for India and others to step up. China and the United States are yet to agree even on 'guardrails' for their relationship, which has steadily worsened over the last two decades. China's internal trajectory and conviction that the United States is determined to prevent its rise suggest increasing, not decreasing, tension within China and externally. The Global South is increasingly disenchanted with the great powers and international institutions, and middle power behaviour has become ever more transactional, following the pattern set by the larger powers. As for world order, pessimistic scholars argue about whether the present world is like Europe before the First World War, or before the Second World War, or is 'neo-medieval'. None of those periods ended peacefully.

It might be argued that international society has the means, the tools, and the knowledge to deal with each of these negative factors. But what tilts the balance in favour of pessimistic assessments is the nature of domestic politics in the great powers and other significant actors in the international system. With new authoritarian and populist leaders in power in several significant countries, mostly isolationist in disposition and dependent on personal charisma and nationalism for their legitimacy, it is hard to see peaceful negotiated settlements emerging to the world's security issues.

The second Trump presidency will likely accentuate US retrenchment trends, global economic fragmentation, the further localisation of domestic politics, and delay moves towards a new global order. These headwinds could simultaneously accelerate the consolidation of local or regional orders, as China is building in Eurasia and attempting to build in maritime Southeast Asia. While US demands on allies and partners will grow, on past performance the Trump administration will concentrate on maximising short-term economic gains for the United

States and could even attempt to negotiate bargains to ameliorate China–US contention. What those policies will be, and whether they will survive the next mid-term elections and contact with reality, remain to be seen, but overall, they raise uncertainty about the role of a United States that is central to Asia's geopolitics. Besides, the increasing use by middle and small powers of the space created by great power rivalry, and the unpredictable and neo-authoritarian and nativist turn of their politics, make it unlikely that we will have coherent or successful international responses to transnational challenges such as climate change and developing country debt. Nor will it make the transition or evolution of a new order easy.

OPTIMISTIC SCENARIOS

Optimists will tell you that never in human history has such a large proportion of humanity lived longer, better, healthier, and more prosperous lives than now, and that the arc of history is bending towards progress. Since the end of the Cold War, the size of the global economy has roughly tripled and nearly 1.5 billion people have been lifted out of extreme poverty. Frank Gavin speaks of our 'historical anamnesis', the inability to properly recognise and accept when circumstances are improving.[14] He argues that there is unimaginable abundance in the developed world, and that today's dangers, some existential, are problems of plenty; that while war will continue, it has changed in nature; and that institutions, policies, and conceptual lenses of past scarcity are ill-suited to meet the potentially catastrophic challenges of an era of plenty. The toxic combination of European industrialisation, social Darwinism, and Malthusian population fears that ushered in decades of imperialism, world war, and deadly revolution between the 19th and mid-20th centuries, is now over.

But does the much larger and increasingly powerful world outside Europe and North America see things this way? Since the 2008 financial crisis, elite opinion in both the richest and poorest countries has become less optimistic about the future and cynical about international institutions. Nor has the international system shown the ability to deal with the grave challenges we face today. It is almost as though the optimists and pessimists see different worlds.

Forced to choose between these scenarios, what might one do? Considering the factors at play, and estimating the likelihood of their coming about, one would tend to see a darker future. But extrapolating from present trends, and discounting human inventiveness and ingenuity, is a form of presentism, the uncritical adherence to contemporary attitudes and concepts. History suggests that we may be in for harder times but not necessarily for the doomsday scenarios that the extreme pessimists lean towards. Humankind has repeatedly faced down or survived disaster and come out better and stronger. We should not expect less of ourselves.

CHAPTER FOUR

India's role

Today, India has a power and influence in the world that it has not enjoyed for several centuries. It is the world's fifth-largest economy and the second-greatest source of growth in the global economy. It has the human and other resources to take advantage of opportunities opened up by new technologies and services. India faces no existential threat and enjoys strategic preponderance on its periphery, though that is sometimes contested. But India also has limitations due to the consequences of multiple partitions of the subcontinent; its under-developed defence industry and reliance on defence imports; difficult relations with its two largest neighbours, Pakistan and China; the overwhelming domestic developmental needs of a poor population; and dependence on the world for energy and critical inputs including technology and capital. Consequently, India must work with friends and partners in the international community if it is to become a modern, prosperous, and secure country. Going it alone is not an option. The choice is between degrees and different kinds of engagement with the international system.

What might India do to prepare for the prospect of a harsher world and continue its transformation?

Independent India adjusted with some success to previous transformations in the international order. It chose to be non-aligned during the bipolar Cold War, working with both blocs and the Global South. In the unipolar moment after the end of the Cold War, India adjusted policy, partially opening its economy, becoming a nuclear power, and transforming its relations with the United States.

Traditional international relations categories such as swing state, balancer, and middle power do not accurately capture India and its place in the world either then or now. Nor has India ever behaved as traditional categories of international relations theory – realism, liberalism, constructivism – would predict. In the decades immediately after independence in 1947, India, despite a lack of hard power, played a significant international role as a normative power, in the delegitimisation of European imperialism in Asia and Africa, in the drafting of global norms such as the Universal Declaration of Human Rights, in the fight against racism and apartheid, in advocacy for conventional and nuclear disarmament, and in the evolution of peacekeeping as an international practice. Through these efforts, Jawaharlal Nehru's India carved out a distinctive place for itself in the changing post-war international order.

As the world situation shifted and India's agency waxed and waned in the international system, the normative impulse in India's diplomacy became less evident. India's foreign and security practice has always been more realist and prudent than suggested by the liberal rhetoric in which it was clothed, and has become more so over time, putting India's strategic and economic interests first.

The stated goal of the present Indian government is for India to be 'a leading power' with a clear vision of how international affairs ought to be organised, not merely a power that accepts the system as it is. India as a *vishwaguru* – a Sanskrit phrase adopted by Prime Minister Narendra Modi that translates to 'world teacher' – is an implicit alternative to the post-colonial Nehruvian vision of India as an internationalist normative power. But so far, the Modi government's normative agenda and direction remain unclear. In three areas – democracy promotion, globalisation and connectivity, and the rules-based international order – the present government is committed to supporting, sometimes with qualifications, the Western-led liberal order, and draws no clear link to Hindu nationalist thought. In climate change and environment, and in the role of religion in mitigating international and civil conflict, there is some connection to earlier Hindu nationalist thinking. So, while the government clearly desires India to become a normative power, it is some way from achieving that ambition.[15]

As in other societies, the question of how to engage the rest of the world has evoked multiple views within India. The traditional answer, since independence, was to concentrate on India's own development and to avoid entanglement in alliances, retaining India's freedom of international manoeuvre. This was the source of the non-aligned policy that others converted into a movement, thus making it more like the Cold War blocs that it opposed. It also opened India to accusations of not pulling its weight in the world. The Nehruvian approach saw India as actively engaged in the world to promote economic development at home. Others, the so-called Hindu nationalists, saw Hindu culture and religion as the appropriate means of engagement, while seeking a much more self-reliant pattern of political and economic development. Their core argument was that if India were to become a prosperous European-style society with Hindu religion, as Swami Vivekananda put it in the late-19th century, the 'civilisation state' of India could bring peace to a troubled world. This is more a vision for the future than an agenda for change in the existing international order.

Unlike Nehru, who saw India as a member of international society and sought to mould that society to India's interests, Prime Minister Indira Gandhi argued that given its unique situation and attributes, India would always be a different sort of power. Indeed, it is hard to think of another power with the same weight, set of internal problems, geography, and stage of development as India. The view of India as an alternative power is one with considerable appeal across the political spectrum in India, leading to a strong sense of Indian exceptionalism. It also feeds into a strong sense of identity that seeks international validation. But history and recent experience show that India does best when engaged with the world rather than trying to go it alone, as it did for a brief period in the 1960s and early-1970s. The high growth years in India, when the largest number of Indians were pulled out of poverty, were the two decades after it opened its economy to the world in 1991.

Now that India has achieved some success in development and created considerable indigenous capabilities, Indians want a larger role for their country on the international stage. This view is particularly popular among the Indian middle class, who read books titled *Why India Is Not a Great Power (Yet)*. Prime Minister Modi, who speaks of India as a world teacher and of India playing a much larger role in the world, is popular with a young and aspirational Indian population. The rhetoric of India's foreign policy has therefore shifted towards much more muscular expressions that play well at home, though its practice shows considerable continuity with earlier caution on important issues.

When it comes to actual state behaviour, there is more continuity than change in India's international role. The stated foreign policy priorities of the present government are a focus on India's neighbourhood first; an 'Act East' policy that centres on Asian engagement; managing China; deepening engagement with the United States, other Western powers, the Indo-Pacific, West Asia, and the Global South; and playing a broader role on the global stage. The Modi government has been particularly active in its outreach to West Asia, working with Saudi Arabia, the United Arab Emirates, and Israel. Together with the United States, it has also committed to an

India–Europe economic corridor through West Asia, working with the I2U2 grouping of India, Israel, the United States, and the United Arab Emirates. In the Indo-Pacific, the Modi government's outreach to islands and neighbours in the Indian Ocean has been noteworthy. Before hosting the G20 in 2023, the Modi government held a summit called the Voice of the Global South, and it succeeded in making the African Union a member of the G20.

Taken as a whole, however, these are not very different from the stated goals and practices of all Indian governments since the end of the Cold War. That is because the fundamental issues facing India remain. India's interests are therefore a better predictor of Indian behaviour than government rhetoric.

If one were to specify those interests – apart from the standard defence of territorial integrity, independence, and sovereignty, and the quest for prosperity – it would lead to a focus on India creating an international environment that enables its transformation. With 40 per cent of India's GDP relying on foreign trade, India has an abiding interest in an open, growing world economy and in India's steady integration into global supply and manufacturing chains. Indian exceptionalism must therefore give way to much more active engagement with the world. This requires working with partners on issues such as energy security and climate change, and continuing to shape the economic environment with partners to the extent possible. India's stand on climate change negotiations has evolved considerably from a defensive one to taking the lead in forming the International Solar Alliance, making voluntary commitments to decarbonise, and so on. Sadly, however, not all choices have proceeded from the reality of India's interdependence with the global economy, such as the decision to leave the RCEP negotiations.

India's transformation also requires an extended period of peace. India will therefore work towards a peaceful periphery extending from the subcontinent to West Asia, the Indian Ocean region, and Southeast Asia, all of which affect India's security and prosperity directly. India's greatest strategic challenge is its relationship with China, with which it shares much of its periphery. There is a conviction in India, based on the attitude to India's quest for a permanent seat on the UN Security Council, that China is the only great power that opposes India's rise.

India also has an abiding interest in forming and supporting issue-based coalitions of the willing and able, as was done with the Quad, I2U2, and BRICS, the last of which has evolved and now includes Iran, the United Arab Emirates, Egypt, and Ethiopia. It is only a range of such groupings that can serve the needs of India's multiple interests. For example, as India's economy grows and becomes more complex, it finds that it is both a major importer of intellectual property rights and increasingly an exporter and originator of them. India therefore works across forums and groups of countries to pursue its interests through issue-based coalitions.

A focus on the Global South will also remain a constant in Indian foreign policy. India is a developing country with a long way to go, and has always found political partners in the Global South. India's non-aligned policy, and the international movement it led to, found support among much of the Global South and was important in the Cold War world. Giving developing countries a voice and a seat at the table, as India did during its G20 presidency by bringing in the African Union as a member, is one way forward. The Global South is India's natural international constituency, given congruence of interests and a common history.

India naturally has a permanent interest in world order issues, but unlike China, India has sought to recast and improve the rules and structures of international institutions to better reflect India's interests, rather than seeking to overthrow or control the order.

Where do the great powers stand on these Indian concerns and interests? The United States has verbally and materially supported India's rise for two decades, and has worked with India to help create a peaceful Indian Ocean periphery. On transnational challenges, there is overlap with the US agenda. If India had to choose between the US approach to climate change (of creating capacity and making renewable energy cheap via the Inflation Reduction Act) and the protectionist EU approach of a carbon tax at the border, India would prefer the US approach. On internet governance, a multi-stakeholder approach that involves industry, consumers, and governments suits India better, as it does the United States. On counter-terrorism, maritime security, and several other issues, India has congruence with the US-led Western approach. The Western order led by the United States seems more conducive to developing India than the vague and worrying alternatives.

One would therefore expect increased Indian engagement with the West while it maintains its strategic autonomy. As India's capabilities increase, it will seek an expanded role globally, but still one that is unique given India's circumstances. What this might translate to in terms of practical policy is outlined below.

THE INDIAN SUBCONTINENT

India cannot prosper alone in a subcontinent that is falling apart, so India's primary focus remains its own region. The present 'polycrisis' among India's neighbours – countries on the subcontinent facing unmanageable debt, recession, civil strife, and heightened geopolitical pressures; in at least six of these countries, governments were changed in the last four years, not all willingly, happily, or constitutionally – offers an opportunity to rework relationships and break out of the unsatisfactory patterns of the past. For instance, connectivity projects are moving ahead steadily with Bangladesh, Sri Lanka, and Nepal. Tense India–China relations have led to much increased Indian attention to its smaller neighbours, Nepal and Bhutan, and this is where one expects greater Indian initiative.

The exception to this cautiously positive outlook remains relations with Pakistan. Since the final US withdrawal from Afghanistan in August 2021, Pakistan's condition has deteriorated and the terrorist threat to and from Pakistan has increased. Now Pakistan, China, and Russia have to deal with an Afghanistan ruled by the Taliban, which they facilitated.

This game has a long way to go. Given the absence of a world order and the great powers' other preoccupations, it is really up to the nations of the Indian subcontinent to deal with their 'polycrisis'. Economically, if these countries and India were to use the crisis to do what we find difficult in normal times, enhancing regional connectivity and cooperation, we would have found opportunity. Connectivity is key – rail, road, power, digital, and other forms. Payment systems could be aligned. Energy, particularly green energy, offers another area with potential. We can draw on the example of India and Bangladesh in the last 15 years, where cooperation on electric power, connectivity, economic linkages, and respect for each other's security concerns enabled a much more successful relationship. That combination of economic openness, security cooperation, and insulation from domestic politics is a useful model on the subcontinent, though not always easy to follow.

South Asians need to work together not just on economic links but also to protect themselves from transnational and other security threats, creating a stable island of growth and development. International politics and the polarisation between the United States and China in Asia creates a chance for South Asians to play a balancing role. For instance, if we wish to secure the seas around us that are essential to our trade and exports, we should be stepping up what India and Sri Lanka started in 2011, working with partners in the Indian Ocean region to improve maritime domain awareness, safety, responses to humanitarian disasters, and ensuring the security of sea lanes. The same is true of other aspects of human security, such as food and energy, all of which polarised Asian politics will not help to solve.

Many South Asian countries are in economic difficulty and face political uncertainty, yet they have a moment of geopolitical and economic opportunity. With the centre of geopolitical contention having come to Asia, South Asia is no longer the geopolitical backwater it was in the Cold War. Nepal is being courted by both China for the Belt and Road Initiative and by the United States for the Millennium Challenge and to sign on to its concept of a Free and Open Indo-Pacific. While the United States is an established presence on the Indian subcontinent, China has recently shown a willingness to involve itself in the internal politics of countries on the subcontinent and to make sizeable investments in them. China brokered unity between the two Nepalese communist parties to bring them to power, offered to mediate between Bangladesh and Myanmar on the Rohingya issue, and has made very clear its preferences in elections in Sri Lanka and the Maldives. China's Belt and Road Initiative commitments to the subcontinent amount to more than US$100 billion. An India–China competition for influence is seen and used as an opportunity by many of India's neighbours, though is still low-key and relatively small in scale.

CHINA

India's biggest strategic challenge is managing its relationship with China and dealing with the consequences of China's rise. The former has to be done with, and sometimes despite, China; the latter will include other powers that share India's interests.

The Line of Actual Control has now been militarised and called into question. This is India's new military reality. Since the 2020 clashes on the Line, both countries frame their dispute as a sovereignty issue, which makes it non-negotiable, only manageable. But neither has yet seriously tried to manage it. After the border clashes, Modi and Xi, who met 18 times between 2014 and 2020, did not meet or speak substantively until October 2024. Both sides are building strength to create a new military equilibrium, but are yet to find one. Now that the dispute has settled into a long-term problem, India will have to undertake a series of self-strengthening steps, if for no other reason than to restore balance on the border. India needs to develop its thinking from preparing for big wars to dealing with smaller applications of force by adversaries. What that means is avoiding a two-front war (with Pakistan and China) by being ready for it; cooperating where possible and competing when necessary with China; and working with others to shape China's behaviour.

India and partners such as the United States have a similar China problem: of trying to walk on one geopolitical leg while lacking the other leg of a coherent and coordinated economic policy because domestic politics prevents it. India and China are deeply economically linked. India–China trade set records in 2021, 2022, and 2023, reaching US$118.4 billion in the 2024 financial year. China is India's biggest source of imports and third-largest export market. India is dependent on China in several critical sectors, a situation that will be familiar to our Australian friends. Chinese value addition in Indian exports has risen from six per cent in 2006 to about 28 per cent in 2023, according to some estimates. India had responded to the crisis of 2020 through external balancing actions and by seeking to lessen its economic dependence on China. These dependencies are considerable in auto parts, pharmaceuticals, electronics, telecommunications, power, and financial technology. India has tightened scrutiny of Chinese investments in India, banned some Chinese mobile apps such as TikTok, and cancelled some contracts with Chinese firms. However, there are limits to decoupling. The Modi government, like Xi Jinping's, has adopted 'self-reliance' as a strategy after the Covid pandemic and economic crash, though it is unclear how much autarchy this will mean in practice. The signs – raising customs duties for seven years running, and leaving the negotiations for the RCEP multilateral free trade agreement, led by China – point to a more insular and protectionist India.

THE UNITED STATES

India's answer to pressure from China, particularly in the last decade, has been to work ever more closely with the United States and others concerned with the consequences of China's rise. The transformation of India–US relations has been the result of steady work by successive governments of widely differing political complexions in both countries. It is something both sides can be proud of. It was achieved despite an imbalance of expectations in the relationship, as well as differing capabilities and stages of development. For the United States, India's primary utility is as a geopolitical tool to deal with China, and secondarily as an economic opportunity. For India, the

United States is an essential partner not just to deal with China, but vital if India is to be successful in its modernisation and transformation.

Today, the relationship faces two shifts: American politics (not just Donald Trump) is turning more isolationist, and the United States expects more from its partners than before. As the United States turns inwards, its utility to its allies and partners diminishes, as does its ability to open its markets and work with partners economically. India and other friends of the United States, such as Japan, have therefore followed a two-fold hedging strategy of hugging the United States ever closer – by tightening defence and security cooperation and commitments, for instance – while increasing cooperation among themselves as protection against US unreliability. Defence, security, and intelligence cooperation has grown manifold in the last two decades among countries in maritime Asia in a belt from Japan to India, through Vietnam, the Philippines, Indonesia, Singapore, and Australia.

INDIA'S CONTINENTAL AND MARITIME INTERESTS

India is both a maritime and continental power. While it works with the United States, Japan, Australia, and others in maritime Asia to keep the peace and sea lanes open and safe, on the Eurasian continent these partners are absent. Here, the available partners are Russia, Iran, and even less promising countries such as Turkey and Pakistan. Throughout Eurasia, China, with Russian acquiescence, is steadily consolidating its economic dominance and increasing its political influence and military presence, particularly in weak nations such as Afghanistan. Without direct access to Afghanistan (thanks to Pakistan's obstruction), India must work with Iran, Russia, and others in West Asia if it is to have any influence in this portion of its periphery.

The consolidation of the Eurasian landmass under new Chinese management is accelerated by Russia's decline and China's alignment with Iran and Russia. The Indo-Pacific framing does not deal with this part of India's security calculus, except indirectly by strengthening Indian capabilities. So, while India's Eurasian partners are, by necessity, those with an active presence, interest, and capability on the continent, in the Indo-Pacific, India works mainly with Australia, the United States, and Japan, but also others such as Indonesia, Vietnam, and the Philippines. As India–China relations have worsened, India's ties with the United States, Australia, Japan, and other partners have strengthened. India and the United States today do many of the things that allies do in defence, security, and intelligence, without a formal alliance commitment to mutual defence.

Australia, the United States, Japan, and other partners in maritime Asia are essential to the transformation of India and the creation of the peaceful enabling environment this requires. They add weight to the growing congruence in approaches to politics and security in maritime Asia. But ultimately, China and the boundary separating it from India is a problem New Delhi will have to deal with itself.

If China–US rivalry has changed the nature of US interest in India, it has also enhanced balancing opportunities for other states, as the Cold War did for the non-aligned. The difference from the Cold War is that, unlike the Soviet Union, China is not a key element of the strategic balance around the globe, yet the United States still is. The United States is an essential partner not just for India, but for everyone else as well. The question is not on the demand side but supply: can US politics permit the sort of global engagement the world seeks?

Does the fact that the United States is critical to India's quest for transformation mean India and the United States should be allies? Not in the sense of defending each other – 75 years after independence, India should be able to look after itself. This would also be asking too much of the United States. Besides, as a global power, US interests are not always exactly in line with India's, as we see in Ukraine and the Eurasian landmass more generally. Where they are, as in the Indo-Pacific (by and large relating to China), India and the United States already work closely together. Foundational agreements in defence have enhanced interoperability, and strategic congruence is growing. Indeed, as India embarks on the self-strengthening necessary to deal with a more antagonistic China and a harsher security environment, it will turn again to the United States as it accelerates military reform. So, while India–US ties may not become a formal alliance, they could increasingly adopt the characteristics of one, short of the commitment to mutual defence that neither side is ready to offer.

INDIA IN ASIA

Today, after two decades of, first, 'Look East' and then 'Act East', India is more engaged with Asia, but not to an extent that satisfies either India or its partners.

Yet if India is to look to Southeast Asia and Northeast Asia for political and security partners, it cannot at the same time walk away from economic cooperation and integration with them. ASEAN will be critical to that effort. The 2020 trifecta of the pandemic, economic crash, and crisis with China has driven India into stressing self-reliance and an attempt to build internal capabilities and cut external dependencies. This makes it harder to cooperate with regional partners who may share India's concerns. This dilemma is reflected in the stop-start nature of India–Australia free trade negotiations, which regained momentum after Prime Minister Modi's May 2023 visit to Australia. India and Australia have had an Economic Cooperation and Trade Agreement since the end of 2022 but hope to replace it with a more ambitious Comprehensive Economic Cooperation Agreement.

The ISEAS–Yusof Ishak Institute *State of Southeast Asia 2024 Survey Report* says that only 0.6 per cent of ASEAN elites expect India to lead in the maintenance of a rules-based order. Confidence in India as a third party to deal with the uncertainties of China–US rivalry is at 10.5 per cent, well behind the European Union and Japan. Overall, while India has enjoyed a significant increase in trust levels (with 24.2 per cent confident it will do the right thing, compared to 16.6 per cent in 2022), doubts about India as a reliable partner are still pronounced (44.7 per cent).[16] India clearly has much to do. I daresay the picture is only marginally different among Northeast Asian elites.

MARITIME ASIA

In the broader maritime domain, India's interest is not in attempting to exclude maritime powers from the Indian Ocean, which is impossible, but to ensure the safety and security of the sea lanes that carry its energy and trade not just in the Indian Ocean but in the seas near China and to India's west. To do so, India must work with all the maritime powers. The larger ones such as China, the United States, and Japan, share India's interest in freedom of navigation on the high seas, and it should be possible for India to take the lead in creating arrangements, formal or informal, that ensure this in India's areas of primary interest.

It is in India's interest to work for open, inclusive, and plural security orders in the Asia-Pacific to replace the present situation of multiple challenges and claims, but China does not make it easy. As China seeks to take centre stage, it could have chosen to work with other powers that share a desire to improve the world order and to concentrate on the economic betterment of their own people. This would have required not just bilateral economic cooperation but addressing the sources of insecurity in the Asia-Pacific, and integrating China into the political and military order of the region just as China integrated itself into global and regional value and manufacturing chains over 30 years. If China had chosen to work for an open, inclusive, plural security architecture in Asia, it would have found willing partners. This has not been China's choice so far. Given its history, experience, domestic trajectory, and recent behaviour, it also seems unlikely to be its choice in the future.

India's role is growing in the informal coalition on China's maritime periphery that has evolved in the last two decades. Defence, security, and intelligence links between India, Japan, Australia, Indonesia, Vietnam, Singapore, and others have greatly increased in quality and quantity. India displays a willingness to work with counties that share its concerns about freedom of navigation and security in this increasingly militarised body of water. The India–US Malabar naval exercises now include others, and a broader security dialogue is emerging that incorporates more than just the Quad members. The security and stability of supply chains in the more difficult economic environment is another issue on which one might expect these countries to work together. At the same time, given the stakes that each has in its ties with China, this informal coalition is probably intended more to increase options than to isolate or act against one country or another.

In this context, India–Australia political and security relations have grown rapidly. Apart from the obvious economic complementarity, India shares Australia's dilemma vis-à-vis China, one that is common across maritime Asia: economies that are structurally linked to a strategic rival. India shares Australia's interest in keeping the Indo-Pacific open, free, and not dominated by any single power. Indeed, there is even 'AUKUS envy' in some circles in India. The two countries are finally beginning to realise the potential in their defence and security ties. Looking ahead, India and Australia might expand their work with others, particularly in cyber, telecommunications, and the undersea domains; the reference to undersea domain awareness during Prime Minister Modi's 2023 visit marked a useful step forward. They could also broaden bilateral cooperation on maritime security in the southern Indian Ocean and the South Pacific. To be even more ambitious, since free trade arrangements are now increasingly difficult, one wonders whether India and Australia could take the initiative to help the Indo-Pacific Economic Framework (IPEF) evolve into an Asian OECD-type norm and rule-setting entity.

With China–US rivalry as the main fault line in Asian geopolitics, it is natural that powers such as Japan, India, Australia, South Korea, Singapore, and others reorient their policies. The standard reaction is to hedge by maintaining relations with both China and the United States, and to simultaneously balance by building up one's own military strength. Long-term US partners such as Japan, South Korea, the Philippines, and Australia have done so by strengthening their ties with the United States. For others, such as India and Vietnam, it is done by strengthening military and security cooperation with the United States while building their own strength and keeping lines open to China. Closer ties with the United States have led India to coordinated action in West Asia for the first time through I2U2. The Quad, the Indo-Pacific Strategy, and IPEF are all part of this rebalancing in maritime Asia in response to the consolidation of the Eurasian landmass by the informal coalition of China, Russia, and Iran.

What we see in Asia is a shifting balance of power as a result of three decades of rapid growth, industrialisation, and militarisation. On the one hand, we are all part of a global economic system – the new frameworks of cooperation in Asia east of India are open, not closed as they were in the Cold War. From a South Asian perspective, the new multilateral bodies attempted in Asia this century are inclusive rather than exclusive, as the previous generation were. Yet Asian politics, internal and external, is increasingly polarised, divided, and fragmented. Therefore, the new frameworks reflect the fluidity and impermanence in the Asian balance of power in their flexible architecture.

The biggest contribution India can make is to manage its own affairs well, and to help the countries in its neighbourhood to enhance their prosperity and security, while working with partners in Asia to keep the region peaceful, open, and not dominated by any single power. This is a situation that calls for countries with common interests, such as India and Australia, to play a greater role in shaping the world.

Acknowledgments

I am very grateful to the editor of the Lowy Institute Papers, Sam Roggeveen, for his patience, help, and ever positive suggestions, without which this paper would not exist or would otherwise have been a much poorer attempt to understand our situation in Asia. The Lowy Institute and its Executive Director, Michael Fullilove, provided the occasion and stimulus for its writing. Research Editor Clare Caldwell provided invaluable support. And I must also thank the two anonymous reviewers whose constructive comments and suggestions vastly improved the paper. But none of them is responsible, as I am, for what has emerged, warts and all.

Endnotes

1 Paul Thomas Chamberlin: *The Cold War's Killing Fields: Rethinking the Long Peace* (Harper Collins, 2018); Graham Allison, 'The Truth about the Liberal Order', *Foreign Affairs*, 28 August 2018, https://www.foreignaffairs.com/united-states/truth-about-liberal-order

2 Hedley Bull, *The Anarchical Society: A Study of Order in World Politics* (London, Macmillan, 1977), pp.8, 13.

3 Xinlu Liang, 'Xi Jinping Hails China Modernisation Miracle as Path for Developing Countries', *South China Morning Post*, 8 February 2023, https://www.scmp.com/news/china/politics/article/3209450/xi-hails-china-modernisation-miracle-path-developing-countries

4 Matt Pottinger, 'The Case for Deterrence: Xi Jinping Wants to Invade Taiwan. The Only Way the US Can Stop Him is by Changing His Calculus', *The Wire China*, 16 June 2024, https://www.thewirechina.com/2024/06/16/the-case-for-deterrence-china-taiwan-xi-jinping/

5 IMF *World Economic Outlook*, April 2015, describes India and China as accounting for 52.77 per cent in PPP terms and 48.99 per cent in nominal terms of Asia's

total GDP. See: https://www.imf.org/en/Publications/WEO/Issues/2016/12/31/Uneven-Growth-Short-and-Long-Term-Factors

6 IMF *World Economic Outlook*, October 2017, https://www.imf.org/en/Publications/WEO/Issues/2017/09/19/world-economic-outlook-october-2017 and World Bank datasets.

7 IMF *World Economic Outlook* and World Bank datasets. See: https://statisticstimes.com/economy/china-vs-india-economy.php

8 Reports on China's first-ever national security strategy, approved by the Politburo in January 2015, included 11 types of security concepts: political, territorial, military, economic, cultural, social, science and technological, information, ecological, financial, and nuclear. Some accounts include ideological security, too.

9 Stephen Roach, 'Global Economic Outlook & Implications for China', a speech delivered to the Center for China and Globalization (CCG), 31 May 2024, citing IMF figures, https://ccgupdate.substack.com/p/stephen-roach-on-global-economic

10 Gita Gopinath, 'How Policymakers Should Handle a Fragmenting World', *Foreign Policy*, 6 February 2024, https://foreignpolicy.com/2024/02/06/how-policymakers-should-handle-a-fragmenting-world/

11 Author's calculations from *IISS Military Balance*, using the methodology in IISS paper on 'Military Expenditure: Transparency, Defence Inflation and Purchasing Power Parity', December 2022, https://www.iiss.org/research-paper/2022/12/military-expenditure/

12 'UN Chief Fears World Headed for "Wider War" over Ukraine–Russia', *Channel News Asia*, 7 February 2023,

https://www.channelnewsasia.com/world/un-chief-fears-world-headed-wider-war-over-ukraine-russia-3258066

13 Robert Jervis, 'Why Nuclear Superiority Doesn't Matter', *Political Science Quarterly*, Vol. 94, No. 4 (Winter, 1979–1980), pp. 617–633, https://www.jstor.org/stable/2149629

14 Francis J. Gavin: *The Taming of Scarcity and the Problems of Plenty: Rethinking International Relations and American Grand Strategy in a New Era* (IISS, Routledge, 2024).

15 Ian Hall, 'Narendra Modi and India's Normative Power', *International Affairs* 93: I (2017) 113–131, https://www.chathamhouse.org/sites/default/files/publications/ia/INTA93_1_07_Hall.pdf

16 *The State of Southeast Asia: 2024 Survey Report* (ISEAS-Yusof Ishak Institute, 2 April 2024), https://www.iseas.edu.sg/wp-content/uploads/2024/03/The-State-of-SEA-2024.pdf

Lowy Institute Penguin Specials

1. *Beyond the Boom*, John Edwards (2014)
2. *The Adolescent Country*, Peter Hartcher (2014)
3. *Condemned to Crisis*, Ken Ward (2015)
4. *The Embarrassed Colonialist*, Sean Dorney (2016)
5. *Fighting with America*, James Curran (2016)
6. *A Wary Embrace*, Bobo Lo (2017)
7. *Choosing Openness*, Andrew Leigh (2017)
8. *Remaking the Middle East*, Anthony Bubalo (2018)
9. *America vs The West*, Kori Schake (2018)
10. *Xi Jinping: The Backlash*, Richard McGregor (2019)
11. *Our Very Own Brexit*, Sam Roggeveen (2019)
12. *Man of Contradictions*, Ben Bland (2020)
13. *Reconstruction*, John Edwards (2021)
14. *Morrison's Mission*, Paul Kelly (2022)
15. *Rise of the Extreme Right*, Lydia Khalil (2022)
16. *Modern Warfare*, Sir Lawrence Freedman (2023)
17. *Best Laid Plans*, Sean Turnell (2024)

BEST LAID PLANS

Sean Turnell

A LOWY INSTITUTE PAPER

The first in-depth account of the economic reform program of Myanmar's ill-fated Aung San Suu Kyi government, by one of her key advisers.

Best Laid Plans is a unique first-hand account of the radical economic reforms implemented in Myanmar under the ill-fated civilian government of Daw Aung San Suu Kyi. These reforms, designed both to turn around Myanmar's dire economy and lay the economic foundations for democracy, were brought to a dramatic end following the military coup in Myanmar in February 2021. Written by one of Suu Kyi's key economic advisers who was imprisoned alongside her in the wake of the coup, *Best Laid Plans* explores the nature of the reforms, the resistance they inspired, and the events that brought this all-too brief era of change to its catastrophic conclusion.

MODERN WARFARE

Sir Lawrence Freedman

A LOWY INSTITUTE PAPER

More than any other modern war, the fight between Russia and Ukraine has been a tough testing ground for modern weapons and operational concepts.

Drawing on extensive research into the conduct of the war during its first year, Sir Lawrence Freedman assesses the contrasting strategies of the two sides. Ukraine has fought along classical lines, seeking victory through battle. Russia has adopted a more total approach, combining conventional battles with attacks on Ukraine's socio-economic structure. Freedman explains why the apparently superior Russian force has been unable to defeat and subjugate Ukraine.

RISE OF THE EXTREME RIGHT

Lydia Khalil

A LOWY INSTITUTE PAPER

ASIO says right-wing extremism now makes up half its case load, and that it anticipates a terrorist attack on Australian soil within the year. There has been a 250 per cent increase in right-wing terrorism globally. So what exactly is right-wing extremism and how is its potential for violence growing? Why is it a global problem? How does it threaten democracy and what should we do about it? *Rise of the Extreme Right* answers these questions while situating Australia within the global threat landscape.

MORRISON'S MISSION

Paul Kelly

A LOWY INSTITUTE PAPER

When he became Prime Minister in 2018, Scott Morrison was a foreign policy amateur confronted by unprecedented challenges: an assertive Beijing and a looming rivalry between the two biggest economies in world history, the United States and China. Morrison plunged into foreign and security policy by making highly contentious changes that will be felt for decades, not least the historic decision to build nuclear-powered submarines.

Featuring interviews with Morrison and members of his cabinet, this book tells the story of the Prime Minister's foreign policy convictions and calculations, and what drove his attitudes towards China, America and the Indo-Pacific.